The Right to Manage?

A study of leadership and reform in employee relations

W. W. Daniel and Neil McIntosh

The Right to Manage?

**A study of leadership and
reform in employee relations**

A PEP REPORT

MACDONALD · LONDON

First published in Great Britain in 1972 by
Macdonald and Company (Publishers) Ltd.,
St. Giles House, 49 Poland Street,
London W.1.

Second impression 1973
Third impression 1973

Printed in Great Britain by
Redwood Press Limited
Trowbridge, Wiltshire

PAPER: SBN 356 04266 9
CASE: SBN 356 04244 8

Contents

Preface

In this report we have set out to highlight aspects of British industrial and employee relations that we judge to be most in need of reform, and to suggest how improvements may be brought about. Our central diagnosis is that the practice of British management has not kept pace with the changes that have been going on around it. It has failed to recognize the implications for management of a changing labour force: better educated, more demanding, more aware of the power it exercises, more affluent, and even in the economic climate of the last few years less threatened by the scourge of high unemployment and in any case insulated from its effects by improved social benefits. Moreover management has failed to recognize sufficiently the implications of parallel structural and technological change in industry; the trends towards increasingly large enterprises, the interdependence of units, higher capital investment and jobs that require less the sheer expenditure of physical effort and more understanding, vigilance, care and responsibility. Such changes place a premium on developing systems of management, remuneration and reward that are designed to minimize interruptions to work and encourage involvement and interest in the job.

Consequently we have focused upon three key areas where we conclude there is the greatest need for reform. First we consider the need and scope for job enrichment, that is the conscious structuring of jobs to provide the greatest possible opportunity for the use of aptitudes, abilities and skills so that work becomes increasingly rewarding in its own right. The second area is the creation of attitudes and institutions that give employees greater opportunity to influence events and become involved in the taking of decisions that affect the carrying out of their daily work, the design of reform and change and in the management of the organization both at plant level and in the enterprise as a whole. Thirdly, we focus on the reform of systems of payment, concentrating on the way in which, apart from its intrinsic value and importance, the introduction of reform provides a specific example of how worker involvement in decision making is necessary to change, and how the operation of the new system provides a basis for reinforcing this. Finally in our conclusions we bring together the main themes of the report and supplement them by considering the additional implications that they have for the management of people.

For analysis, diagnosis and prescription we employ four main research methods. First we draw upon two detailed case-study analyses of workers' evaluations of collective agreements in which they have been involved. This enables us both to develop a general explanatory framework of the relationship between the worker, his job and his employer, and to identify a spectrum of differences in these relationships. Secondly, we extract relevant findings from our study of sixty collective agreements that were brought about by the productivity criterion provision of the incomes policy operating from 1967 to 1969. These we term the 'productivity criterion cases'. Thirdly, in cases in which employers have taken initiatives relevant to our analysis we have sought these out, talked to management, workers and trade unionists and used the results for illustrative purposes. For instance, the ICI weekly staff agreement was a major set of changes, based upon a very similar diagnosis to our own of what was wrong with employee relations and we therefore refer to it extensively. Fourthly, we present findings and conclusions from other research that has been carried out in employee and industrial relations.

The study was financed by a grant from the Leverhulme Trust and carried out within the framework of a major programme of research in collective bargaining for change backed by the trust. The research was carried out and the report written by W.W. Daniel and Neil McIntosh. A PEP Advisory Group, composed of employers, trade unionists and specialists in employee relations, made a major contribution to the study. Interviewing was conducted by the authors, Tony Beck and Will McQuillan. Susan Martin acted as secretary to the study, and typed successive drafts of the report.

PEP is grateful to the Leverhulme Trust for its generous backing, to the members of the Advisory Group for their careful reading of drafts and valuable help and suggestions, and to the managements, trade unionists and workers who co-operated so freely with us in our research.

Section One

Job Enrichment

1 The case for job enrichment

If there is one single lesson that can be learned from all the management innovation and basic research on people and their jobs over the last ten years, it is that the tasks employees are required to do in their work are of central importance in influencing their attitudes to both the job and the organization for which they work. In particular it is increasingly being recognized that if the content of an employee's job holds no interest for him then he can hardly be expected to take any interest in it. If it provides no scope for responsibility then he can hardly be expected to act responsibly. If it provides him with no opportunity for exercising the basic human need for some control or influence over his actions and environment then he will seek to recover some control in ways that are damaging to the efficiency of the enterprise: by restrictive practices; restriction of output and taking pleasure and satisfaction in sabotaging and defeating the procedures through which management seeks to exercise control over him. And above all, if his job gives him no opportunity to use and develop his abilities in achieving a result that has some meaning for him and with which he can identify, then it is hardly surprising if he regards his work, his place of work and everything associated with it with hostility or resignation as an aspect of his life to be endured in order that he can begin to live outside work.

Of course there is nothing new in this diagnosis of the human condition in industry. The impoverishment of work through mechanization and mass production has been consistently identified by social critics as a source of social and psychological evil ever since the industrial revolution. What is new is the extent to which the diagnosis is now coming increasingly to be shared by managers and

3

businessmen. They too are beginning to recognize that the arrival of comparatively full employment, the emergence of a better educated workforce, and the improvement of social benefits now mean that there are limits to the economic benefits that can be achieved through the fragmentation and rationalization of work in a way that treats the operator as an appendage of the machine. People can no longer be treated as dispensable units of labour, bound to fulfil whatever tasks management requires of them and easily replaceable if they do not. For instance, among the economic and managerial benefits assumed to flow from breaking work down to its simplest components, and organizing it so that any individual operator performs only one very simple task, are that it means that unskilled labour can be utilized, the training period is short and training costs low, and any operator is readily dispensable and easily replaced in event of absenteeism, sickness or labour turnover. A recent report on the electronics industry, however, which studied in particular women wirers and assemblers, found that labour turnover was reaching levels of up to 81 per cent, and calculated that these levels of labour turnover were costing the industry about thirteen million pounds a year (Wild and Ridgeway, 1971). Moreover contrary to popular management mythology this labour turnover was not mainly a result of women leaving to get married or have children. The majority quit not because of domestic circumstances but because they could not tolerate the dreary and depressing nature of the work and the lack of opportunity for them to use and develop their abilities. There was no scope for personal achievement or recognition of their efforts.

The nature and effects of fragmented work

Most of these women were working on simple, assembly-line jobs and it is the assembly line which has come to symbolize the impoverishment and dehumanization of work in the twentieth century and given rise to pathological consequences for people, and for organizations. Assembly-line production has required men to shed their most human qualities at work. It has prevented them from using or developing their aptitudes, abilities and intelligence. It has required them to fulfil a mechanical link in a mechanical system, a link as yet too complex or expensive for the engineer to automate but a link that remains sub-human to the extent that the level of intelligence required is such that it can readily be matched by the middle and higher orders of animal life.

The operation workers are required to fulfil is a routine, repetitive one closely defined by the mechanics of the technology. The pace, sequence and frequency of tasks are wholly dictated by the technical design of the line. The isolated task has no meaning in terms of any complete operation or product. There is no satisfaction in a job completed; no finished product to symbolize achievement. Men are tied to the same place on the line. As long as the line runs, work is not over and the assembly line rarely stops. Activity is but activity and perpetuates only itself. It has no meaning and does not interest, involve or engage the worker.

In this way assembly-line work is taken to epitomize an alienating industrial environment. Workers have no say over the how, why, where and when of their activity. They are powerless appendages of the machine. They perform a fragmented, isolated task and are deprived of any insight into an over-all design. Work is meaningless. They are excluded from any involvement in collective endeavour by the break-up of industrial work groups and by the coercive nature of relationships with supervisors and managers. They are socially isolated. They are enduring activity, which is essentially a source of intrinsic deprivation for purely extrinsic rewards. They are self-estranged. (Blauner, 1960)

From this, it is argued, flow a number of damaging consequences that are as predictable as they are observable. Employees are alienated, dissatisfied and hostile. At the individual level this leads to absenteeism, sickness and can in extreme cases be associated with mental breakdown, psychological disorder and even a greater propensity to embrace totalitarian political philosophies such as fascism. At the collective level it leads to a high level of conflict which is ultimately represented in the way that vehicle manufacture, within which the assembly line is the predominant technology, has one of the worst strike records in UK industry.

This total argument is a very persuasive one in that it has internal consistency and makes sense psychologically, and each part of it can be backed up by reference to selected research findings. At the same time it is certainly not a complete picture for it clearly owes much to the social and occupational values of those who advocate it. They include social critics, social science researchers and progressive managers, who are all inclined to assume that everybody wants the same out of their job as they do. Because they place a high value on interest, responsibility and the opportunity to use their abilities creatively in their jobs, and be recognized for doing so, they cannot conceive how anyone else can endure a job that does not satisfy such values. Clearly people with a wide range of abilities, opportunities, social and occupational experiences and in different economic and social circumstances, have a wide range of priorities in what they seek from their jobs. Thus it is never safe to assume that one's own priorities are the same as everybody else's. Even if it were true that all people sought job interest, congenial working relationships, high remuneration and good working conditions from their jobs, they would still be likely both to attach different relative values to these requirements, and to define them in different ways.

Equally what people expect from their jobs owes a great deal to what they have learned they can reasonably expect. They have an enormous capacity to make the most of the possibilities open to them and be in some sense satisfied with the result. Thus surveys asking people how satisfied they are with their jobs tend consistently to come up with the finding that the large majority express at least moderate satisfaction. This may no more than reflect the reality that during the early period of their working lives people tend to change jobs relatively frequently until they find something that is generally tolerable, or until family responsibilities which restrict their mobility, force them to become reconciled. They come to tolerate jobs devoid of meaning and interest through lack of opportunity to do anything different.

For these reasons it is hardly surprising that some studies of motor-car assembly workers have come up with conclusions suggesting a rather different picture from that of the worker so frustrated and embittered by personally destructive work that he is hostile and antagonistic to all around him.

In particular a survey by John Goldthorpe and his colleagues at the Vauxhall works, Luton, suggests that once you take into account the question of what different groups of people are seeking from their job, then a pattern of work which is recognized and experienced as total deprivation can exist quite happily with high ratings of satisfaction with job, supervisors and employer. (Goldthorpe *et al.*, 1970).

This study argues that the key to an understanding of the auto-assembly worker's responses to his work and workplace is the question: what is he looking for from his job? The researchers found that the operators in their sample had sought the job voluntarily, even eagerly, and they had sought it overwhelmingly because of the high financial rewards it offered. They had often given up jobs that were richer in intrinsic rewards, interest, responsibility and the opportunity to use skills and abilities, in order to take on the assembly-line job. Equally they were generally aware of alternative jobs they could find which would be richer in intrinsic rewards but they preferred to stay where they were because of the higher level of remuneration. Moreover they gave a generally high rating of satisfaction towards the job, towards Vauxhall's and towards their supervisors, because the job and their employer rewarded them highly in terms of the only aspect of the job where they sought rewards.

Thus, the study concludes, here was a group of workers with a particular and distinctive set of priorities in what they sought from work. Because of a particular set of social experiences or a particular stage in their family life-cycle, they overwhelmingly attached primary importance to high earnings, and saw their work and their workplace in purely 'instrumental' terms as a means to an end, where they would experience deprivation in return for extrinsic rewards, and not as an end, or a source of rewarding experience, in its own right. Thus, in taking on this particular kind of work, they had implicitly made a contract. They had voluntarily and consciously accepted a particular kind of work, knowing what it involved, in return for a level of earnings higher than any they could find elsewhere. As long as the employer honoured his side of this contract by continuing to pay these relatively high levels of earnings, they were content. This congruence or consistency between what they sought from their job and what it furnished explained the high levels of satisfaction with the job and with the employer, and also Vauxhall's relative strike-free and trouble-free, labour-relations experience, compared with that of other auto manufacturers. The men, of course, experience the work itself as deprivation but because this was consistent with their expectations, because they had accepted this as part of the contract, it did not create frustration and spill over into generalized aggression and hostility towards everything associated with the job and the work place.

This analysis very effectively explains why this particular group of workers sought, accepted, endured and were relatively content

with jobs which to many other people seem quite intolerable. When
the analysis goes beyond explanations of job choice and lack of job
changing, its conclusions do, however, become more debatable, but
we shall pick these up in Chapter Three when discussing needs,
priorities and motivations in different situations and contexts.
Meanwhile these findings underline again both the way in which
different groups of industrial workers have different priorities in
what they seek from their job, and the importance of locating any
analysis of the behaviour of a particular group of workers in the
context of what they themselves seek from the jobs rather than
imposing one's own set of values upon them.

Similarly the conclusion of a study by Turner of labour relations,
disputes and strikes in the UK motor industry attaches less
importance to the technology of production and the impoverished
work this demands, than to variations in the market for motor cars
and fluctuations in demand for them. (Turner *et al.*, 1967)

These two different types of finding demand caution in explain-
ing behaviour purely in terms of a particular type of technology and
the implications this has for the quality of job content. Nevertheless
it remains true that certain patterns of attitude and behaviour are
strongly associated with particular technologies and that this can be
directly traced to the scope that jobs within these technologies
furnish for interest, autonomy, control and the use of abilities. Thus,
if we take assembly-line work at one extreme and craft work or
continuous process work at the other, there are variations in intrinsic
job satisfaction, involvement and feelings of responsibility which are
reflected in absenteeism, sickness and turnover rates. We can
certainly say that assembly-line work is experienced as deprivation
by operators, and that it does contribute to a low level of
involvement in the job.

For instance the following account of work on semi-automated
petro-chemical plant is unlikely to be echoed by an assembly-line
worker.

It's the ABC of this industry, responsibility. I like it. If I leave the
job there could be danger – there could be fire – there could be
thousands of pounds worth of damage. We couldn't walk off the
job – you feel responsible for your mates and for the job. That's
why there's never any strikes – you never hear of any strikes in this
industry – it's the responsibility. It's like policemen, nurses and

doctors – you never hear of them going on strike – they're in so much of a circle – they've got so much responsibility. It's the same in this job – the more responsibility you've got the less you think about things like striking.

Thus while one must not attribute all the ills of the motor-car industry to the job content determined by the technology, if one thinks in terms of a set of underlying or predisposing factors, coupled with a possible range of trigger incidents as causes of any particular social behaviour or event, then the quality of work is clearly one of the predisposing factors that give large parts of the motor industry a hair trigger that can easily and quickly be activated by a range of different incidents. At the same time it is clearly only one factor among many, including the systems of payment and grading; fluctuations in the market and the consequent insecurity; uncertainty and variations in relative management/labour strength; grievance procedures, together with their speed and effectiveness; and management attitudes, practices and policies.

Some suggested solutions to fragmented work

We can however see that the pattern of working and job content of assembly-line work do contribute to a number of damaging consequences for both the employee and enterprise, and the poverty of the jobs here are all too characteristic of other sections of industry. There have been a number of remedial policies and practices advocated to prevent or moderate the damaging consequences of fragmented, rationalized work. The first of these is the pure 'human relations' solution which argues that the damaging effects of the work itself can be alleviated by developing rewarding, supportive and meaningful human contact and interpersonal relationships. Thus supervisors and managers should be trained and encouraged to be sensitive to operators' feelings and needs as individuals, to give them support and encouragement and to reassure them that they are important and human despite the fact that the tasks they do and the role they fulfil in the organization are such as to suggest the exact opposite. Similarly they should be given the opportunity for social satisfaction through friendship and social contact within work groups. The chief problem with this solution is that there is strong evidence that, in a situation where already they have so little autonomy, freedom and discretion, all that many workers demand of supervision and management is that they be left alone. Thus rather than valuing supportive management contact, they resent it as yet a further encroachment upon their independence. (Goldthorpe *et al.*, 1970) There may well be variations among different types of workers in response to this approach however, and some may find such supportive, 'human relations' contact some palliative for the deprivation of the job.

The second solution is to provide 'satisfaction substitutes' of a different kind through the best possible physical working conditions, amenities and such diversions as piped music, but these clearly can never be more than palliatives.

Thirdly, it is suggested, following the line indicated by Goldthorpe's findings, that attention should be focused on devising means of selecting employees whose personalities and orientations are most appropriate to this kind of work. Again, while clearly it makes good sense for management to try to ensure the best fit between recruit and job, there are two very questionable assumptions in this prescription. The first of these is that, at any stage in the development of technology, the chief determinant of the human characteristics required of industrial workers, there is a fundamental congruence between the distribution of skills, aptitudes and expectations of people in the labour market and those required in the jobs available. To take the square peg and round hole analogy: the shapes of people looking for employment must be perfectly matched to the holes that industry has to offer them. All that management has to do is fit the right shape to the right hole. One of the basic themes running through our report is that this is not the case: that increasingly the aptitudes, education and expectations of workers are outstripping the demands made by the jobs that industry is able to offer. Indeed this assumption is intrinsically unlikely to be valid in so far as, while it would be difficult to argue that the innate distribution of basic aptitudes or innate potential has varied within the population over centuries, the distribution of jobs available in the economy demonstrably has. Moreover this prescription is essentially conservative, mechanical and unconstructive, representing the blind alley that occupational psychology entered some forty years ago by focusing on fitting the worker to the job rather than paying attention to the job, or the organization of tasks and enquiring how these might be changed to fit them to the needs of the worker.

Equally unconstructive is the fourth answer offered which accepts that there is a basic incongruence between the needs which workers bring to work and the jobs that industry has to offer, but suggests that the problems that this imbalance generates are something that management has to learn to live with. This view holds that when the quality of work is such as to make it pure deprivation and pure disutility it is wholly unreasonable to expect that employees will be involved or identified with what is a source of pain. It is only reasonable to assume that they will regard their work, place of work and management with hostility.

The only solution in these circumstances, it is suggested, is to reduce the possible sources of conflict to a minimum: by introducing systems of payment which will not cause disputes, institutionalizing the remaining causes and by teaching management to live with uncertainty, difficulty and dispute and not seek ineffective panaceas. Within this solution there is, at least implicitly, the suggestion that management and the economy will increasingly have to accept strikes, disorders and overt conflict as part of the costs that shareholders and the community have to bear in exchange for what workers suffer in large industrial enterprises where the system of organization and quality of work strips them of all opportunities for control and self-expression. While there may be an element of truth in this proposition it is equally true that it would be more constructive to try to reduce the costs for both the worker and the shareholder and community.

It is this possibility which is suggested by the fifth alternative advocated, that of restructuring and re-organizing tasks to inject some interest, meaning and reward into them through 'job enrichment'.

While all these prescriptions are not mutually exclusive and while management in different types of situation may find something in each of them which is of value, it is the 'job enrichment' prescription which is the most positive, creative and constructive, and which therefore warrants the most serious consideration in terms of its rationale, feasibility, scope and limitations.

The contribution of Herzberg

The idea of 'job enrichment' has by now, of course, become inextricably associated in the public mind with the name of the

American psychologist Herzberg. In fact both the concept and the practice of job enrichment predate Herzberg and, ironically enough, he rejected the idea as impracticable (Herzberg, Mausner & Snyderman, 1959) in his original work. Subsequently he has become a convert to what his followers, disciples and interpreters have found in his work, and his original enquiries effectively and dramatically highlight the case for job enrichment, should it be feasible, and also provide an attractive theoretical link between attitudes or job satisfaction and behaviour and performance.

The key to Herzberg's whole research and motivational theory, and the originality of his contribution, lie simply in the questions he asked in his surveys. He' posed these key questions: What are the events, situations or circumstances in people's jobs that give them personal satisfaction? The second key question was the opposite: What are the sorts of event that make people dissatisfied? He went on to ask people to recount events of the two different types and describe their feelings during and following these events. He found that the two sets of episodes that emerged did not represent opposite ends of a continuum but rather constituted two distinct entities. Sources of positive satisfaction tended to relate very much to the actual *content* of people's jobs, the tasks they performed and the responsibilities they carried in doing their jobs and the way that these were appreciated by people whose judgement they valued. Five main types of event emerged:

Achievement: when workers had been able to complete a task which represented a personal achievement; they had done something in which they could take pride and satisfaction

Recognition: when their performance and achievements had been praised, complimented, approved and rewarded

Responsibility: when an especial degree of trust had been invested in them; they had been thought capable of accepting a particular responsibility which reflected a recognition of their abilities and personal characteristics

Advancement: when they had been promoted or moved on to new demands, responsibilities and challenges

Intrinsic interest: when the tasks they were doing were particularly interesting in themselves

Essentially these types of particularly satisfying events and associations can all be seen to relate to opportunities for self-expression and self-actualization. Employees had been given an opportunity to express and develop their own personal interests and abilities; they had been gratified by the result and they had been even more gratified if this personal satisfaction was reinforced by the approval and respect of others.

When the dissatisfying episodes were analysed very different patterns of events emerged. These tended to relate to the working conditions and situation, the job *context* or environment rather than the work itself. Such events included: occasions when pay or remuneration were thought inadequate or inequitable; physical working conditions unsatisfactory; personal relationships with super-ordinates, colleagues or subordinates disagreeable; working hours inconvenient; fringe benefits unsatisfactory; or finally company policy out of line with the respondents' ideas.

Thus when something was seen to be wrong with the working environment, it became a source of dissatisfaction, but removing the source of dissatisfaction did not create positive satisfaction in this regard. The dissatisfaction merely ceased to be an irritant and its absence was taken for granted. If you have a stone in your shoe it is irritating, even painful, but once it is removed you quickly regard it as normal, proper and unexceptional not to have a stone in your shoe.

From these findings and his analysis Herzberg deduces the motivation to work. He argues that if you want employees to be interested and involved in their jobs, if you want them to be positively motivated to improve their performance, then it is unproductive to confine your managerial activity to improving working conditions and relationships. If pay is low or the system of payment is unjust, if working conditions are dirty, unsafe and uncomfortable, if personal relationships are poor, and so on, dissatisfaction is very likely to result, reducing both motivation and performance. But excising such sources of dissatisfaction will succeed only in raising motivation and performance from the low level to which it has been depressed, to a neutral level of instrumental compliance. Employees have a right to expect working conditions to be safe, clean and human. If they are not, then employees are properly aggrieved. If the source of grievance is removed this is properly taken for granted. Thus in situations of ideal physical and social working conditions, the best that can be expected is that employees will be relatively content and will do what is required of them without resentment, though without interest and involvement.

To raise interest, involvement, motivation and performance above this level, it becomes necessary to provide jobs that are rich in intrinsic rewards; jobs that provide scope for achievement, recognition, responsibility, advancement and interest; jobs that furnish opportunities for personal satisfaction, self-expression and self-actualization. Where such rewards are not naturally or spontaneously generated by the jobs, then it becomes necessary to restructure them to inject interest and meaning by job enrichment.

As we shall see in Chapter Three particularly, this theory is quite inadequate as a total theory of occupational motivation. Moreover it may well be that job enrichment is not feasible or would prove uneconomic for large sectors of industry and the economy. Again it may well be that working conditions, systems of payment and interpersonal relationships are so bad in large sectors of industry, that there is an enormous volume of work to be done to raise activity and performance even to the hypothetical neutral level. Until that has been achieved, it is grotesque to talk of job enrichment, positive involvement and motivation.

Nevertheless Herzberg's approach does dramatically highlight the importance of job content and, taken with our account of the damaging effects of routine, repetitive and rationalized work, underlines the importance of making jobs as rich as possible. Moreover there have been some interesting and valuable attempts to apply these lessons. In describing some examples of work structuring for greater interest and involvement in Chapter Two, and in seeking to put these into context in Chapter Three, we distinguish between three orders of change: job rotation, job enlargement and job enrichment:

Job rotation is the lowest order of change and refers to the practice of changing people from one job to another within a work group so that although the individual jobs they do remain as devoid of interest and personal demands, at least they experience some variety and relief from the routine in doing a number of different jobs.

Job enlargement is the next order of change and refers to the horizontal extension of jobs so that, although once again the individual tasks any particular operator does may require no greater skill than before, he has a larger and more diverse task repertoire.

Job enrichment is the highest order of change and is sometimes called vertical job enlargement. It refers to the structuring into jobs of higher levels of conceptual thinking and responsibility so that, for instance, operators are taking decisions that were formerly the prerogative of supervisors.

2 Some examples of job enrichment

The promise implicit in job enrichment that it can reverse what seem to have been inexorable trends in the development of mechanization and replace the modern wage slave with the historical ideal of the free, creative craftsmen is powerfully attractive to many. They tend eagerly to seize on any hints and signs that this has been achieved. Thus one often hears a statement such as, 'Philips have done this' followed by a catalogue of resultant achievements. But when the Philips' experience is examined more critically it turns out to be distinctly more modest in scope and effect than has been imagined. In this chapter we report on three published accounts of attempts to apply the principles of job enrichment, and systematically monitor and evaluate the results.

We should introduce here a further note of caution. Many of the examples we now report were originally presented as if they were closely controlled scientific experiments. But the reporters and investigators are often job enrichment missionaries not only in the sense that they are socially and intellectually committed to the concept but also in the career sense that they are trying, as internal or external consultants, to sell job enrichment to business and management. This is not to suggest that they consciously set out to produce findings that could be distorted to suit their case but natural scientists working under laboratory conditions can be unconsciously led by their hopes and expectations to see and select what they want to find, and miss and ignore what they do not like. Accounts of field studies in the behavioural sciences undertaken by the committed must be approached critically. It may well be that the roles of dispassionate investigator, apostle and salesman can be sustained simultaneously but the sceptic's evidence is more

16

persuasive than the believer's. Nevertheless these cases do provide hard examples of what is involved in the practical application of job enrichment and evidence of the effects its application has on attitudes and performance. Later in Chapter Three we attempt to put these effects into perspective.

The Paul/Robertson ICI experiments

The first series of cases that we summarize are derived from Paul and Robertson's report *Job enrichment and employee motivation.* (1971) The authors report a number of experiments undertaken within ICI, involving a number of occupational groups: sales representatives, design engineers, experimental officers, draughtsmen, production and engineering foremen, toolsetters, process operators, fitters and operatives. In each case small experimental groups were set up, and their jobs restructured to inject more responsibility, discretion and autonomy. The changes in performance and intrinsic job satisfaction of the experimental groups were measured and related to those of control groups who were subject to no change but selected to match the experimental groups in both composition and circumstances.

Sales representatives

Changes in the jobs of this experimental group all aimed at enabling more personal decisions to be made on patterns and frequency of calling on buyers, reporting, seeking technical support, pricing and complaints. Representatives were no longer required to write reports on every customer call, but instead to pass on information or seek advice or action as they themselves thought appropriate. Representatives were given direct access to the technical services department, which agreed to provide service 'on demand' and to treat calls as their first priority. This replaced a system by which requests were channelled through intermediaries. Responsibility for deciding frequency of calls was placed wholly on the representative for him to judge what was appropriate for a particular customer. Representatives were given discretion to make immediate settlements of up to £100 in cases of customer complaint. Similarly, if faulty material had been delivered or if the customer was holding material for which he had no further use, the representative had complete authority to decide how best to deal with the matter and was empowered to buy back unwanted stock even if it was no longer in the company's selling range. Perhaps most importantly, representatives were given a discretionary range of about 10 per cent in the prices of most products sold.

An experimental group of fifteen salesmen worked under these new arrangements and their performance and attitudes were compared with the rest of the sales force over the same period. During the trial period the experimental group increased its sales by 18.6 per cent compared with the same period of the previous year while the sales of the control group dropped by 5.0 per cent. The gross profit margin per pound of products sold by the experimental group was as high as that of the control group, so clearly the experimental group's higher sales volume did not reflect a tendency for them, on average, to use their 10 per cent discretion to charge lower prices.

Job satisfaction in the experimental group increased by 11 per cent and in the control group by less than 1 per cent.

Experimental officers

This exercise started with low morale in the research and development department, among experimental officers (EOs) whose job was to implement experimental programmes devised by graduates. As non-graduates, their career prospects were limited but at the same time they felt that their experience and technical ability were being wasted. The chief aim of the exercise was to give them more scope to exercise their abilities within the existing organizational hierarchy.

This was attempted through the following changes. EOs were encouraged to write a final report on each project for which they had been responsible. The minutes carried the author's name, were issued with those of the scientist, and the author was fully responsible for answering any query arising from it. Officers were more involved in the planning of projects and experiments and given time to follow up their own ideas even if these went beyond the initial research outline. They took part in interviewing candidates for laboratory assistants' jobs, acted as first assessor on their own assistants and were made responsible for devising and implementing a training programme for junior staff. They were empowered to requisition materials and order services on their own signature. Two experimental groups of fifteen and fourteen officers were set up, and their performance compared with a control group of fifteen over a period of twelve months. Variations in performance were evaluated by superiors' assessments of monthly reports (requested from all groups for the first time) and by the number and quality of minutes produced. After an initial period in which the performance of both experimental and control groups rose, that of the control group fell away while the experimental groups sustained their improvement.

Production and engineering foremen

A point to which we return repeatedly in our report is that the growth in size of enterprises, the development of specialist professional services and techniques in production planning and control, personnel recruitment, training and control, industrial relations and production engineering, have all consistently eaten away at the autonomy, responsibility, authority and influence of the foreman. Thus while management pays lip service to the idea of the foreman as the linchpin in management structure, the first line of management playing a critical role in mediating the policies and philosophy of the enterprise in face-to-face contact with shop-floor employees, all that this often means is that troops are sent into the front line without any ammunition. They become frustrated, ill-equipped and unmotivated to represent management as it would wish. For instance our own enquiries have clearly revealed how, where organizations have given workers and work groups greater autonomy in day-to-day working and greater involvement in management decision-making, foremen have tended increasingly to see themselves as 'errand boys', 'messenger boys' or even 'tea boys'. They are sandwiched and powerless between two self-sufficient groups: on the one hand, the operators who know more about the detailed peculiarities of the plant and its operation than they do, who have increased decision-making powers at that level and want nothing more than to be left to run the job as they know best; on the other hand, the professional managers, engineers and service specialists who are taking all the higher-level decisions. If this erosion of the functions and discretion of the foreman is as widespread as all the signs suggest, then few changes are more important to the health of the enterprise than the redefinition and enrichment of the role of the first-line manager. This may reduce the number of nominal supervisors and change the qualities needed in them.

In their studies Paul and Robertson set up two experimental groups, one consisting of twenty-three production foremen and the other of twelve engineering foremen. In each case the changes designed to give more responsibility to foremen were very similar. They were assigned special projects such as the improvement of quality control. Middle-management offices were resited to become physically more separate from the work-place, so that foremen had more 'on the spot' autonomy and there was less temptation and opportunity for middle management to interfere continuously in relatively routine operating decisions. Production foremen interviewed and selected candidates for jobs within their own work teams, and made all decisions on non-standard payments. All foremen were given ample disciplinary authority over workers under their command, short of the power of dismissal, and all were given formal responsibility for the assessment, training and development of their subordinates. The experimental period ran for six months.

Assessments of the performance in relation to control groups showed markedly higher ratings among the experimental groups and impressionistic assessments suggested that the growth in the responsibility of foremen had led to disputes being settled more quickly and effectively. Training and assessments became more effective and the contribution that the foreman's special experience can make to the solution of long-term organizational and technical problems was more effectively harnessed. It also emerged however that, while some foremen blossomed and developed rapidly under their new responsibilities, others were quickly exposed as unable to cope with the new system. This underlines how important training and selection are if substantial new demands are to be made on people.

Other groups

As indicated, similar studies were set up with design engineers, draughtsmen, toolsetters, process operators and fitters. The aims in each case were very similar: to analyse job content and job descriptions in such a way as to identify the extent to which responsibility could be delegated down the line and the content of jobs built up. Design engineers were given more control over their own budgets and the recruitment, selection, appraisal and salary reviews of their staff, and the choice of consultants for special projects. Draughtsmen were organised into multi-skill teams allocated to particular projects which they saw through from beginning to end. They were more concerned with costing and design. They were better briefed about the projects on which they were working. The shop-floor studies were less systematic and extensive and add little to those described in the remainder of this chapter and the next.

The AT & T studies

A very similar series of studies was conducted in the Bell System, a subsidiary of the American Telephone and Telegraph Company, and reported by Robert N. Ford in *Motivation through the work itself.* (1969)

Nineteen trials were conducted on different sites covering jobs as varied as those of semi-skilled, shop-floor workers, clerks, professional engineers, keypunch operators, switchboard operators, service representatives and complaints representatives. In each case experimental groups were set up with radically restructured job descriptions and the effects on technical measures of performance, employee attitudes, and customer and managerial attitudes were monitored and compared with those collected for control groups. Over 2,000 employees were involved in the studies. In only one application, perhaps significantly a shop-floor-worker trial, was the over-all evaluation 'not successful' while the remainder were rated at least 'modestly successful'. As the approach adopted and the changes made were in many ways very similar to those of the Paul and Robertson studies there is little virtue in describing each case in detail.

One application that does warrant particular consideration, however, because it illustrates a shop-floor example well, is the case of the 'framemen'.

They were a group of forty men engaged in the wiring up of telecommunications frames. The initial procedures and organization were as follows. An order was taken for a particular piece of work by one of a group of craftsmen who translated the order into the framework to be done. This order was then passed on to one of the teams of three into which the forty framemen where divided. One worked at one end of the frame soldering wires to the frame. The second ran the wire to a third man soldering to a frame at the other end which was elsewhere in a huge building. Subsequently their work was checked by a circuit-test group. Thus there was a high degree of both specialization and fragmentation. There were three distinct and specialized functions: taking orders and design of specifications; wiring the frames; and testing the circuits. Moreover, within these separate functions there was further fragmentation as can be seen from this description of how the three-man framemen teams worked.

There had been much trouble with this group of men and a history of low output, missed completion dates, poor quality and faulty work, high overtime and a catalogue of grievances expressed by the men through their union.

A plan for change was devised, aimed ultimately at integrating all the formerly discrete components of the job. The first stage was to integrate wiring and testing so that a test man was substituted for a cross-connection man in the wiring team and the team became responsible for both completing the wiring of the circuit and testing that it was adequate. The second stage was to link the team directly to the customer so that the team received the order direct, did the write up and turned the working circuit over to the customer.

This proved to be one of the most successful trials. It illustrates the different aspects of the process of enrichment well. First came analysis of the components of the job and how these were organized. Then work and work team were reorganized and a meaningful module of work tackled rather than a set of separate, fragmented tasks. The longer-term effects of the changes were to bring about a dramatic reduction in those failings of the group that had been such a source of concern to management. Orders were completed on time where previously only some 50 per cent of completion dates had been met. Quality standards were consistently met. Grievances dropped off sharply.

The Philips experience

Most of the applications in the first two published reports that w‚e have looked at were confined to either white-collar jobs or skilleu‚ manual jobs. Such occupations are, however, very different from those on the highly mechanized assembly line. The largest single volume of work structuring with the aim of greater job interest and satisfaction among manual workers doing this type of light assembly work was undertaken by Philips in Holland and reported in *Work structuring – a summary of experiments at Philips*.

There were two main social aspects of the firm's initiative. The first, as with the ICI change programme, was the recognition that social relationships within industry had not kept pace with changing social attitudes and values outside industry; and, equally, that the quality of job and task that people were given within industry were incongruent with the needs, capacities and expectations they had developed as a result of being better educated, better informed and more demanding.

Secondly, Philips found themselves with a chronic labour shortage at the beginning of the 1960s when they recognized that they had to take substantial steps to make the work they offered more attractive in order to attract and retain labour. They diagnosed that in their industry one of the prerequisites of making jobs more attractive was to inject more interest and meaning.

The programme of change that they devised as a result of this diagnosis included three distinct phases. The first was the 'work environment', nicknamed 'the flower box', seen purely as a stage of short-term palliatives during which management could make some concrete, physical demonstration of its interest in improving working conditions. It changed the physical environment by such means as more effective and acceptable noise, temperature and humidity control; cleaner and better canteen, working and lavatory facilities; and improved protective clothing and better facilities for relaxation.

But, as indicated, this stage was seen only as one in which they could, quickly and relatively easily, tangibly express the managerial will to make improvements, but without any expectation that this would produce anything more than a short-term improvement in working atmosphere. It was further recognized that it would be necessary to build on this foundation quickly by work structuring of jobs, if any longer-term benefits and improvements were to be achieved.

This gave rise to the second phase, which was concerned with directing attention to restructuring production systems in a way that would increase social and personal satisfactions. Because of Philips' policy of decentralizing management and the high level of autonomy this gave local management, the actions during this next stage were diverse, and uneven and met with varying results. It would have been quite inconsistent with the over-all management philosophy to cevise a standard programme of change that could have been applied uniformly and evaluated systematically through the units and plants in the group. Rather it was a matter of indicating a certain direction and leaving local management to work towards that direction in ways that were most appropriate to their circumstances and resources. Consequently a very patchy picture emerged, with some local managements embracing the concept of job enrichment enthusiastically and working towards it wholeheartedly, drawing on professional services, both technical and social scientific, to help in the design of the changes and the evaluation of the results, while others did very little. In between there was a spectrum of variations.

This meant that Philips gained very varied and valuable experience of different methods of approach, different ways of introducing change and different organizational and production systems. But it also meant that this experience was gained in a very unsystematic, sporadic and *ad hoc* way, with no opportunity for rigorous analyses of the costs and benefits of the programme throughout the company. Indeed it is probably true that, even had they wanted to, it would have been impossible to draw up a meaningful balance sheet for the whole programme. It was difficult enough to evaluate individual initiatives in comparatively simple and well defined contexts, but there was also the problem of evaluating the effects of an enormous programme in a context of changing technical, economic and social frameworks. Indeed there are so many changes in initiatives of this type — social relationships within work groups and between them and management; systems of payment; physical conditions and layout as well as job content — that it would be difficult to identify the contribution of the different components even if it were possible to establish the costs and benefits.

What is clear is that a vast number of initiatives were taken, which ranged from simple job-rotation and job-enlargement initiatives to much more ambitious and profound job-enrichment exercises. Examples of job enrichment included one in which 100 operators, working on a traditional continuous conveyor belt with a five to ten second, single and repetitive, job cycle, were reorganized into small relatively autonomous, product teams. Each team of eight to ten operators was responsible for all assembly tasks involved in the manufacture of a particular product. Job cycles were extended, on average, to between ten and twenty minutes, and even to more than an hour. The group took over many of the former responsibilities of supervisors, inspectors and maintenance and service departments. For instance, groups were made responsible for carrying out simple maintenance themselves or bringing in skilled fitters where jobs were beyond their scope. Groups organized their own job rotation in so far as it was appropriate to the abilities, interests and preferences of group members. The group had a working group leader and two levels of supervision were removed from the old, formal, structured, vertical system. This type of very radical innovation required a high level of collaboration between line managers, production and design engineers, supervisors and behavioural scientists, as well as the operators themselves.

Some initiatives resulted in striking improvements in quality and output as well as in increased job satisfaction as expressed in labour turnover, absenteeism and attitudes towards management. Equally, other initiatives produced somewhat disappointing results.

Philips' management has drawn the following conclusions from their experience:

Top management. Here the 'degree of change that can be achieved is related to the level of the highest man interested'. This underlines the importance of getting top management committed to the initiatives and identified with their success, though it does not follow that once top management is convinced, it can introduce this type of change single-handed. Top management should not necessarily be the agent of the changes. It may well be that a co-ordinating group on which the different groups and specialisms we have identified are represented is a more effective agent of change. But any such body is unlikely to be successful unless it knows that it has the wholehearted backing and support of top management, which must be seen to be committed to the changes from the start.

Middle management and supervisors. These were among the groups most resistant to the changes. It becomes clear when shop-floor organization is altered that any form of production system relates not only to technical and financial matters but is also an expression of managerial attitudes, ideology, and assumptions about the goals, interests and motivations of workers. The old, vertical, hierarchical organization set above a fragmented work system with operator behaviour controlled by the carrot and the stick is based on what McGregor terms the X theory of employee motivation and behaviour. (McGregor, 1960) Managers and supervisors are not involved in this type of organizational system and cannot operate it for a number of years without beginning to embrace the ideas and values that it represents.

Problems arise when organizational changes are made, for the ideas about worker motivation and behaviour that lie behind job enrichment initiatives are often in direct opposition to the assumptions behind the traditional structure. Thus when concluding a successful and radical reorganization, it is not enough for top management or a specialist co-ordinating committee to direct its attention to the changes that can be made on the shop floor. Any such changes are unlikely to fulfil their goals unless the attitudes and associated practices of middle management and supervisors change in a way appropriate to the new organization. This requires a high level of both formal training and the involvement of management and supervision at each stage of the change process.

What this highlights, too, is that job enrichment cannot be implemented in isolation from the rest of the organization. Changes in the managerial and supervisory hierarchy mean that less supervision and fewer supervisors will be required. A more fluid, organic horizontal structure will be needed, as opposed to a static, mechanistic vertical one. This underlined the need for what Philips saw as their third phase (although with hindsight they would probably recognize that it should have been an integral part of the work structuring phase), which they term the departmental structure phase, based on the principle of organization from the bottom upwards.

While it is easy to represent the reservations and lack of co-operation of supervisors and junior management as a reflection of the ways in which the new ideas run counter to their prejudices, it is also clear that they have more direct and obvious grounds for doubt in this type of reorganization of which the chief is redundancy. In Philips this arose in two ways: fewer low-level supervisors were needed and at the charge-hand level it is very difficult to redeploy people out of the line into staff jobs. It seems clear that for many charge-hands at Philips the only alternative open was to be downgraded as operator in other departments.

The second redundancy threat which supervisors recognized was in terms of redundant skills and functions. While it may be possible to enrich and build up the jobs of lower management in the way described in the Paul/Robertson case, it has still to be recognized that unless this is carried out as an integral part of shop-floor job enrichment, lower management will be asking themselves where they will be at the end of it all — and are unlikely to be committed to the changes, or to carry out their role.

Operator involvement. The basic assumptions of job enrichment and departmental structure, based on the principle of organization from the bottom upwards, demand a high level of operator involvement. While recognizing the importance of this, Philips stuck mainly to the standard procedures through the works' councils and on-the-job consultation. But this is a theme that we take up much more fully in Section Two with some very impressive examples of involvement for change with reference to job enrichment.

There were marked variations of desire among operators for more varied, larger or richer jobs. The chief sources of such variations were age and sex and there was a tendency for younger women in particular to prefer the simple, routine jobs where they could develop an automatic rhythm, have no need to concentrate and feel free to gossip or enjoy piped music. Some forms of job restructuring tended to break this rhythm, demanding attention and concentration without giving any compensating reward in terms of increased interest and satisfaction. This was particularly the case in some applications of rotation and enlargement. Indeed the scope for the application of job rotation in a way that is gratifying to operators seems to be confined to small work groups that can be left to devise their own patterns of work sharing and rotation, according to the interests and preferences of group members.

Market pressures. The effect of market pressures could be seen in two main ways. First, as we have noted, the critical shortage of labour at the end of the 1950s and beginning of the 1960s had been one of the chief sources of the felt need to improve jobs to make them more attractive both to current and potential employees. Secondly, the economic climate changed in the mid-1960s towards one of partial recession. This put the pressure very much more on cost reduction and cutting back. Management became less concerned with making jobs attractive than with tightening up. The job enrichment programme lagged and there tended to be backsliding. S pervisors who had moved into more service-type roles in relation to work groups tended to slip back into their traditional authoritarian roles. Moreover as the cutting back was associated with the period following the work structuring programme there was more disaffection with job enrichment on the part of employees as it began to be seen as 'just a new way of getting rid of people'.

The way in which progress towards the objective of the job enrichment programme ebbed and flowed in response to market pressures might suggest that it is a luxury that can be indulged in good times but which is dispensable when the going gets rough.

This is not a conclusion to which Philips would subscribe. They would, however, accept that when a long, painful process of organizational change is in train, there is a tendency for management to relapse into the old, familiar, easy habits when the pressure is on.

Above all the Philips experience emphasizes the need for an integrated approach to organization change. The pursuit of social goals on their own while technical and financial considerations are ignored is likely to prove as self-defeating as the sole pursuit of technical or financial goals. One of the most impressive characteristics of the whole Philips programme is the way it attempted to bring together the social, technical and economic.

3 Job enrichment in context

In Chapter One we made out the case for job enrichment and in Chapter Two reported examples of the application of its principles to a wide range of different types and levels of job. We demonstrated that job enrichment is widely feasible and that it can bring manifest benefits to workers and to management. Now we seek to place both concept and practice in context in three senses: by reviewing just how practicable job enrichment is for the mass of blue-collar jobs and workers; by assessing the nature and extent of the benefits that can realistically be expected to follow from applications in those situations where it is appropriate; and by locating the meaning of job content in the social and economic frameworks that are often equally if not more important aspects of workers' jobs. This process of review, and what will essentially be qualification, is necessary as we have detected among some managements a tendency towards quite unrealistic expectations of job enrichment which are unrelated to the reality both of technological constraints and, more importantly, the priorities and interests, of industrial workers, particularly in terms of how they can effectively bring about their own economic advancement.

Fallacies about job enrichment

Though we do not wish to be too unfair, we can illustrate many of the fallacies about job enrichment by reference to a recent pamphlet *The Wages of Fear* dealing with wage-led inflation and incomes policy. (John Nelson-Jones, 1971) Here it is argued that boring jobs and lack of job satisfaction are one of the chief sources of wage inflation. The majority of industrial workers have to endure demoralizing, repetitive jobs, which make them frustrated, aggressive, envious and greedy. Consequently they both join trade unions and put in outrageous wage claims to compensate for their lack of jou satisfaction. Thus boring jobs directly contribute to wage-push inflation both by direct stimulation of wage claims and by strengthening, in terms of both membership and support, the position of trade unions. Their collective bargaining position is strengthened and they are consequently better able to achieve inflationary pay settlements.

The author concludes that if only Government would initiate a programme of job enrichment throughout industry, making every job interesting, rewarding and responsible, then everyone would be satisfied and content, lose interest in trade-union membership and activity and forget to put in pay demands.

The danger in this type of analysis is not only that it is naive and impracticable but also that it is likely to be positively harmful, exciting resistance from workers and trade unionists to innovations such as job enrichment because they see them as inspired by a managerial ideology directed towards weakening union strength and depressing industrial earnings. Again these are not views put forward by just one pamphleteer. The ideas and assumptions behind the analysis are shared by many apparently well intentioned managements, who often see job enrichment as a means whereby they might overnight transform militant, organized, industrial workers into contented, compliant staff, no longer attached to ideas of collective protection and advancement through trade unionism. Similarly they have sometimes seen 'job enrichment' as a means of introducing labour flexibility by the back door, under the cover of a more seductive title, and bringing increased job satisfaction for the worker. Breaking down traditional demarcation between different groups of craft workers on the one hand, and between craft and general workers on the other, in order to utilize labour more effectively, has been a widespread objective of many managements in British industry during the last ten to fifteen years. This, however, has normally been pursued quite openly within the framework of productivity agreements which have rewarded workers with a share of the increased productivity ensured by a better labour utilization. For management consciously to try to achieve the same objectives by calling the changes 'job enrichment' and not by increasing workers' remuneration according to their new responsibilities can only result in suspicion of management, charges of 'manipulation', resistance to future changes, and the bringing of the idea of job enrichment into disrepute. This would be a grave loss because job enrichment does have a great deal to offer workers and trade unionists as well as management. Indeed, as we go on to discuss in our consideration of means of making the trade union more effective as a channel of representation and involvement for workers, job enrichment is something which unions should strenuously advocate and strive for. The quality of the work their members do and the level of their job satisfaction should be one of their prime concerns, for trade unions, in seeking to represent the interests of their members and maximize their rewards, should increasingly turn their attention to the aspect of work which is often least rewarding: the work itself. In principle they should be particularly concerned about increasing workers' control which is exactly what job enrichment seeks to do: increase workers' control over their day-to-day work activities, an area in which they can be seen to seek and value autonomy and control spontaneously. But where management and its spokesmen are advocating, and seeking to use, job enrichment as a tool to weaken unions and workers' influence and bargaining strength, it is hardly surprising if they become suspicious of, and hostile to, innovations that could be of benefit to all parties. In fact workers have no real need for fear. Management has no hope of achieving those goals we have attributed to its more ill-advised representatives via job enrichment. Because their members' jobs have been made more interesting, trade unions are no less likely to pursue, nor have any less support from their members in pursuing, wage demands related to the cost of living, the earnings of other sections of the community or the profitability of the enterprise. This can be readily illustrated by the way in which at each socio-economic level it is often in practice the groups with the most interesting and rewarding jobs, the greatest responsibility and the highest status, who have the most powerful collective organizations, exercise the most rigid unilateral job regulation and pursue their economic and occupational interests the most single-mindedly and effectively. Examples are skilled craftsmen among industrial workers and lawyers and doctors among white-collar workers.

The relationship between job enrichment and collective bargaining is well illustrated by two case studies of productivity bargaining that we reported in *Beyond the Wage-Work Bargain*. (W.W. Daniel,

1971) These confirm that intrinsic job satisfaction and job enrichment have very little impact upon worker strategies and attitudes towards management in formal collective bargaining, and tney suggest that while effective job enrichment could, within the framework of the social reorganization that we advocate in Section Two, contribute to the more orderly and rational conduct of labour relations and collective bargaining, it is by no means likely to reduce the vigour with which workers and their representatives pursue their interests. This is particularly so when they see their interests to be in conflict with those of the management.

The case studies refer to workers' evaluations of productivity agreements in which job enrichment played a direct or tangential part. We describe and discuss productivity bargaining in more detail in Chapter Five, where we highlight the lessons of enduring value that the practice holds for collective bargaining. Here it is sufficient to say that, essentially, productivity bargaining involves the renegotiating of methods of working at the same time as renegotiating rates of pay in relation to the increased responsibility, workload and savings in labour cost brought about by the new methods of working.

Job enrichment and collective bargaining: the case of the petrochemical operatives

The first case we looked at was a classic productivity agreement of the type common in continuous-process plants such as oil refining and heavy chemical production. As well as illustrating the significance of job enrichment in relation to collective bargaining, the case also shows how job enrichment can be brought about spontaneously and tangentially through the pursuit of other objectives. Because, historically, work impoverishment has been strongly associated with mechanization and technically more efficient and economic systems of working, it is often assumed that the direct pursuit of more efficient working must necessarily be in conflict with the idea of more interesting, rewarding tasks and jobs for workers.

In this case more interesting and rewarding work was generated spontaneously by a set of changes whose prime concern was the better utilization of manpower, in the quite mechanical sense of that term. The group of workers we studied were the process-production operators.* As far as they were concerned, the agreement sought a reduction in manning; more flexibility among operators so that they would carry out a wider range and level of tasks over a broader span of the process (including some simple maintenance tasks); a simplification of the grading system by the substitution of five basic grades for the nineteen different rates of pay previously operating; a slight reduction in the seniority rules; and a stable forty-hour week with no overtime or additional payments. The men's share of the savings thus brought about included increases in pay ranging from £4 to £6 a week, which represented proportions ranging from 15 to 30 per cent, and conditions of employment more akin to those of staff employees, which included a guaranteed annual salary paid weekly, full pay when sick and an end to clocking in.

Relationships in the plant between management and men and between supervisors and men were excellent, reflecting the mutual respect and reciprocity characteristic of those in continuous-process technology. Despite this, the changes sought in the agreement were fiercely resisted it appeared through retrospective interviewing largely because the agreement was seen as a threat to security of employment and job opportunities, despite the fact that it carried a no-redundancy guarantee. Indeed, the reduction of job opportunities in the local labour market that resulted remained the chief source of any residual hostility towards the agreement even nine months after it had been introduced. Thus the agreement was initially greeted with hostility and resistance and it was only pushed through eventually on the basis of tough bargaining over the men's share of the savings in terms of increases in earnings and fringe benefits, in relation to the new skills they would have to learn and the new responsibilities they would have to carry.

We interviewed the men nine months after the agreement had been accepted. At this point there had been a complete change. The large majority of men now favoured the agreement and, more surprising than this reversal of their general attitude towards it were the reasons that they now gave for approving it. These are summarized in Table 1.

*Details of the sample and interviewing are reported on pp.43 and 52 of *Beyond the Wage-Work Bargain*.

Table 1

Reasons for favouring agreement (base: all informants)

	%	No.
Greater job interest/satisfaction (intrinsic rewards)	68	33
More opportunities to use ability/ do wider range of jobs	(33)	(16)
Work generally more interesting	(20)	(10)
More opportunity to learn different jobs	(13)	(6)
More responsibility	(3)	(1)
More money	30	14
Better conditions of employment	26	12
Promotion seniority systems better*	(15)	(7)
Wages secure—full pay when sick	(5)	(2)
Clocking ended	(5)	(2)
Other	9	4
Working team bigger	(3)	(2)
Social equity—incomes policy good for low-paid workers	(3)	(1)
Company's competitive position	(3)	(1)
Total	133	63

*Including those who had benefitted personally under the agreement.

As Table 1 shows, the most frequently mentioned items related to the job enrichment that the agreement had spontaneously and tangentially brought about. The most commonly mentioned sources of satisfaction were the ways in which the changes in working practice defined by the agreement had made work in the plant more interesting and satisfying by giving operators more chance to use and develop their abilities through learning and carrying out a wide range and higher level of job — both simple maintenance tasks and operating jobs covering a broader span of the process. The following are typical comments:

You got stuck on a unit — you got used to the job — it was just repetition — your mind didn't have to work — you were in a rut — since the new agreement you have got to keep thinking all the time — you have got more scope, more variety, more to do — there is more interest — you have got interest in three plants not just one.

The scheme itself is good — men will stagnate if left on one plant for years and years — it is good when you get a chance to do different jobs and to learn different jobs — if you are here for eight hours you might as well be working for eight hours as getting bored doing nothing half the time.

You are more flexible now — before you were confined to just one job — now nobody is indispensable — you are not stuck for ever on one job — the more people that know the job the easier the running, the safer the job and the more interesting it is.

Over two-thirds of the sample spontaneously mentioned this type of item. The second most frequently mentioned item (cited by 30 per cent of informants) was increased earnings. Third was better conditions of employment, which included those who felt they had benefitted personally under changes in the promotion, seniority or grading systems, those who emphasized that earnings had been made more secure, and those who welcomed the end of clocking in. Other items mentioned, by one or two people only, were that incomes policy and productivity bargaining helped the lower-paid worker, that they had become a member of a larger work team and that it had helped the company's competitive position.

Particularly interesting is how the changes in conditions of employment and fringe benefits, designed to represent a substantial move towards staff for the men, hardly featured at all among their reasons for now approving the agreement. We shall return to this point in our conclusions when discussing staff status and conditions of employment.

But certainly the most striking and interesting aspect of these findings is that factors related to job interest and satisfaction were those most frequently mentioned — by 68 per cent of all respondents. The proportion is more than double those spontaneously mentioning 'more money' despite the fact that every man interviewed had received a pay increase of at least 15 per cent and most had received increases nearer 30 per cent. Indeed the proportion mentioning items related to job interest or satisfaction exceeds those mentioning all other items including money.

Here we have a strange paradox. The agreement had been negotiated and implemented in the face of strong opposition and only after hard wage-work bargaining backed by a national incomes policy. Yet nine months after the agreement, the majority of the men favoured the changes because of job enrichment, heightened interest and satisfaction in their work rather than because of increases in wages. Managers and even trade unionists who have engaged in hard productivity bargaining will find it hard to believe that workers may be more interested in intrinsic job satisfaction than in increased wages.

The point, of course, is that in the negotiating context they were not more — perhaps even not at all — interested in job satisfaction. They wanted to make the best deal in the terms that the negotiating context defines: increased earnings in some currency in relation to increased responsibilities and work load, with clear reference to the social and cultural implications.

But once agreement had been reached and once the changes had been implemented, the formal benefits that it had furnished were taken for granted and what then became important were the changes that had been generated in the context and meaning of their day-to-day activities and relationships at work. In practice this meant that there was virtually a complete reversal in priorities when the reference point was the work rather than the negotiating context.

All too often when people think about work attitudes and motivations they think in terms of a fixed set of priorities, needs or interests. They ask 'What is the worker really interested in?' with the assumption that he is interested in the same thing to the same degree in all contexts. Thus one answer that has increasingly worked its way into management thinking is that suggested by Maslow and popularized by McGregor that man and the worker have a need hierarchy. (Maslow, 1970: McGregor, 1966) Man is a wanting animal with an ascending order of needs. As one is satisfied, so it ceases to be salient, ceases to motivate as it no longer exists as a manifest need. At the bottom of the hierarchy are the physiological needs: food, shelter and security. Then follow the social needs: group membership, acceptance, approval and belonging. Ultimately come the ego needs: to find and express oneself, to create, to use and develop one's abilities.

According to McGregor's popularization of these ideas in relation to the industrial worker, industrial society has largely satisfied all the lower-order needs. The industrial worker now has all the food, shelter and security that he requires. His social needs are largely satisfied too. Being satiated, these now cease to operate as needs but the hunger that remains unsatisfied is the hunger for self-expression and creativity. This is what the worker is now really interested in and this is what industry should be giving him if it wants him to be motivated and involved. Thus, by a different route, McGregor comes up with a very similar answer to Herzberg in terms of the priorities and motivations of the industrial worker.

But there are alternative, very different answers. One that we have already hinted at is offered by Goldthorpe. (1970) His starting point is that to know what the worker really wants of his job look at the critical decisions he makes in his occupational life. Look at his job choices and his job changes. Study his behaviour, as well as his attitudes, in terms of the characteristics of the jobs he seeks, the jobs he takes, the jobs he quits and the jobs he rejects. As we have seen, when he applied this approach to his study of car workers he found that what the worker was primarily interested in was earnings. It was the relatively high level of remuneration that attracted men to the job, that made them give up intrinsically more interesting and rewarding jobs to take it, and that kept them in it when there were other more intrinsically rewarding jobs that they could have taken. Thus Goldthorpe concludes that if you look at what needs workers bring to the enterprise as a result of their social experiences, and relationships outside work, if you examine what they do when they come to the crunch of choosing between one job and another, then you will find that there is plenty happening in our consumer society to keep Maslow's lower-order needs fully operative and to ensure that workers attach a very high order of priority, if not the highest, to earnings. In this way these alternative approaches give us a completely different set of answers to our question 'What is the worker really interested in?'

On the one hand, there is the suggestion that affluence in industrial societies has created a situation where the primary concern of workers is the lack of opportunity for creative activity in work rather than the further increase of their material wealth. On the other hand, there is the conclusion that the advertising, consumer economy, on which the wealth of the advanced industrial societies is based, creates an insatiable demand for consumer goods, which in turn ensures that the economic motive in work remains paramount and will remain paramount for the foreseeable future. But, while offering directly contradictory conclusions, each of the approaches described shares the common assumption that the worker has an ordered and consistent set of needs or priorities in what he seeks from a job; that this set of priorities is reflected and manifested in all aspects of his work behaviour and choices. It is this basic assumption that our data question in this case. The answer, our findings suggest, is that the worker is interested in many different things in different contexts and circumstances. If we look at attitudes to the agreement at the negotiating stage then it seems that Goldthorpe's conclusions on workers' priorities is justified.

But if we look at their assessment of the agreement in the operating stage, the McGregor/Herzberg diagnosis of worker motivation seems more valid. Thus because they were interested in very different things in the two different contexts their evaluation of the self-same agreement, involving the self-same set of changes, differed dramatically at different points in time. Both answers to the question of the workers' real interest can be seen to be valid—but partial because they confine themselves to his interests in only one context.

The way that priorities vary with context can be further illustrated by reference to the replies of men on three other key areas of motivation in the same study. What was it that attracted them to the job? What satisfaction did they experience in the job? What reasons had they had, if any, for ever considering leaving the job? Replies to these questions revealed that generally security, pay and working conditions had attracted them to the job in the first instance; that the opportunity to use their abilities in problem resolution was the chief source of satisfaction on the job; and that the lack of opportunity to progress up the seniority grades because of the very low labour turnover predisposed those few, who were not firmly entrenched, to leave. Again, while the criteria on which job-choice decisions were made reveal an instrumental set of priorities, attitudes to the job itself show a very different set.

Thus, in terms of understanding workers' behaviour and attitudes, the critical question is often not the one so frequently posed of *what* are people really interested or most interested in or *whether* they are more interested in job satisfaction and intrinsic rewards than money and extrinsic rewards, but rather, *when* are they interested in intrinsic rewards and *when* are they interested in extrinsic rewards.

Just as our findings on the petro-chemical workers' evaluations of their agreement showed that priorities in what was sought from the job varied from context to context, so they demonstrated too that attitudes towards management, and images workers had of the basic

relationship between management and labour, varied in much the
same way. To simplify, the men generally felt in the negotiating
context that management and men were on opposite sides and their
respective interests in conflict, whereas in the work context there
was a greater tendency for them to feel that they were working with
management in concert as a team. This variation in attitude according to context is again something that many managers find hard to
grasp. They assume that the attitudes expressed in one context are
characteristic of attitudes in all contexts. They demand complete
loyalty and identification with assumed common interests and in the
absence of complete loyalty and full identification assume total
opposition. And yet recognition of both different and common
interests, is essential to the health of a pluralistic, hierarchical organization and has profound implications for forms of worker representation and involvement in decision making. We therefore return
to the theme of variations in attitudes to management in our next
section.

Here we can extend our analysis of how priorities in what is
sought from the job vary from context to context, and the implication this has for the practice of job enrichment, by looking at our
second productivity bargaining case, in which job enrichment played
a major part. This highlights how the failure to distinguish between
what workers are interested in in different contexts has led to some
misunderstanding of the significance of Herzberg's findings. Because
his form of questioning reveals that, for very many types and levels
of employee, the chief sources of positive satisfaction in their work
lies in the scope that it provides for achievement, interest, responsibility, recognition and advancement, management has often assumed
that workers would welcome changes calculated to increase this type
of reward. They have assumed that if they could devise productivity
agreements that allowed for an element of job enrichment then
workers would be attracted to them for this reason.

The findings of our first case demonstrates the weaknesses of this
thinking. Although the agreement did bring about job enrichment,
and although the changes in work content were subsequently
experienced as gratification, it was only within the framework of
collective bargaining, and the different priorities that are salient in
that context, that the agreement was made possible. Moreover just
because that agreement was subsequently experienced favourably, it
by no means meant that further agreements were welcomed and

enthusiastically embraced when first proposed. Indeed, what management saw essentially as two tidying-up agreements were subject to the same hard negotiation as the first.

Similarly, at the individual level, it is not always true that a job that is richer because it demands more use of abilities will be attractive from the outside. The prospect of such a job may even be threatening and worrying. For instance there was evidence in the first case that many of the older men were far from attracted by the prospect of increased demands on their abilities, and the training they would need to fulfil these demands. They were worried that they would not be able to cope with training and that they would not meet the increased demands. All other things being equal, they would have preferred to have continued in their own quiet way, doing tasks that were familiar to them, which if they had become relatively unexciting and uninteresting, were also undemanding. And yet having been required to make the change, they found the fact that they had been able to cope very gratifying, and very often found the new method of working more interesting and satisfying.

The case of the nylon spinners

Our second example of workers' evaluations of an agreement again confirms the fallacies inherent in assuming that the promise of heightened job satisfaction will play a major part in attitudes to a formal agreement at the negotiating stage. This case refers to the application of the ICI Manpower Utilization and Payments Scheme (MUPS), later restyled the Weekly Staff Agreement (WSA), at its Gloucester nylon spinning plant.* We describe this agreement, its aims and effects more fully in Section Two. Here we are primarily concerned with the job enrichment component. As well as broadly confirming the pattern that emerged in the first case and our analysis of that case, this example had three other major characteristics that are very relevant to our theme in this chapter.

First, the primary technology of the nylon spinning works is

---

* For our account and analysis of this case in *Beyond the Wage-Work Bargain* we were grateful for access to the results of interviewing carried out by Clive Vanplew at the works, and which we draw on again here. These have now been published in full as *The Nylon Spinners.* (Cotgrove, Dunham and Vanplew, 1971)

more akin to the assembly line than the continuous-process technology characteristic of oil refining or heavy-chemical production. Thus, whereas 85 per cent of the operators at the petro-chemical plant had found their job interesting at least most of the time, here, by contrast, 80 per cent said that the job had been 'very' or 'fairly' monotonous before the agreement. Indeed the men complained that the most unsatisfactory feature of the job was the boredom of their tasks and the way that time dragged so that they went home tired and listless, not because they had had to work too hard but because they had been dulled by the routine, repetitive nature of their tasks. (Cotgrove, Dunham and Vanplew, 1971)

Secondly, this case involved massive participation by shop-floor workers and trade-union representatives in the design of the changes. This degree of involvement was critical to the whole exercise and indeed the changes were built on it. The chief channel of worker involvement was shop-floor discussion groups in which all operators as well as supervisors and shop stewards participated. These had three main purposes. First the nature of the national framework agreement of which this was a local application was explained to the men. Then the benefits it was hoped workers would get from restructuring of work content in terms of enhanced job satisfaction were outlined as were the increased earnings and improved conditions that would represent their share of the savings brought about by more effective labour utilization. Finally the groups were designed to throw up the men's ideas about how jobs might be reorganized in order to make for both more efficient operation and interest. According to the evaluations of both management and men these group discussions were very productive and we discuss their nature and effectiveness more fully in our consideration of worker involvement in decision making in Chapter Five.

Thirdly, as indicated, the exercise was consciously designed to bring about job enrichment as an explicit objective, rather than a tangential spin-off as it proved to be in the petro-chemical case. It is probably fair to say that this was one case where management expected that the prospect of increased job satisfaction, through greater responsibility, autonomy and control, would be a major attraction of the agreement, and management was at pains to sell this attraction in the groups.

In essence the changes in working practice and organization thrashed out through the discussion groups and joint working parties

were consistent with management's original aim of moving away
from a situation where men were working on simple individual jobs
motivated by the carrot of financial incentives and the stick of close
supervision, to one where they were more self-motivated and
exercised self-control. This was done by removing one level of
supervision, and instead establishing work teams responsible for a
group of machines, and giving them more discretion over manning
machines to ensure good, continuous operation without constant
reference to supervision. The more fluid and flexible system of
working that the men themselves devised permitted reductions in the
level of manning of the order eventually of 25 per cent, as well as a
work mix and task structure that did indeed give the men the greater
job satisfaction that it was designed to do.

However, in view of management's clear intention to incorporate
job enrichment into the changes, and its expectation that the chance
of more intrinsically interesting jobs would be a major attraction of
the agreement, it is interesting to look at the men's retrospective
ratings of how they evaluated the agreement before it was
introduced, compared with their evaluations when it was in force.

Operators were asked what, if anything, had attracted them about
the agreement initially. Forty-two per cent mentioned increased
earnings alone, 25 per cent increased earnings coupled with a factor
related to job interest, and 33 per cent said there was nothing in it
that had attracted them. Thus, despite all the beneficial effects of
the involvement discussions and the way that job interest featured in
these, it was the promise of higher earnings that was the chief, if not
the only, attraction of the agreement. For only a quarter of the men
was the promise of greater job interest at all salient at the
negotiating stage and, even for them, it was very much a secondary
item. Since the men were interviewed after the changes had taken
place and after they had experienced the resulting increase in job
interest, it is reasonable to suppose that their replies if anything
overstate the interest that they originally felt in increased intrinsic
rewards. Certainly it is clear that it was only on the basis of the
re-negotiation of the wage-work bargain in a way that offered
increased earnings and improved fringe benefits that the changes
were made possible. This is not to say that the offer of higher
earnings on its own would have been sufficient to bring about the
degree of change that was achieved as smoothly as it was. As we
demonstrate in the next section the opposite is likely to have been

the case, but in practice it was the promise of higher earnings that was the basis upon which all else was built.

However, as in the first case, while the initial attraction of the agreement was confined to the promise of more money, once again after the changes had been implemented there was a marked change in attitudes to the agreement and in reasons for approving it. Once again it enjoyed a wider range of support for a wider range of reasons. At the time of interviewing 75 per cent of the men said they felt more satisfied with the job as a result of changes the agreement had brought about (the feelings of the residual 25 per cent were unchanged). Of the 75 per cent experiencing increased satisfaction, 12 per cent felt this was only very marginal and referred spontaneously only to the increase in earnings but the remaining 63 per cent felt that they had experienced more substantial benefits: greater job interest through wider areas of activity and responsibility, more rewarding relationships with work-mates through membership of groups working together, and more freedom from supervision.

Direct questioning on changes in level of co-operation, autonomy and job interest produced these responses:

First, as a result of the organization of men into larger work groups with corporate responsibility for a number of machines and ending the payment-by-results scheme, 72 per cent of the operators felt that co-operation among the men had increased. Not only did they welcome this (over 80 per cent attached considerable importance to getting on well with people at work) but they could also see jobs being done that had been neglected before and that people were at hand to help in case of difficulties. Management observed how the men themselves devised intricate patterns of job sharing and rotation that kept both them and the machines working in ways that would have been impossible to design or impose from above.

Secondly, 88 per cent of the men said they felt they were subject to less supervision in their work since the agreement. Once again not only did they see this freedom to get on with the job in their own way as a benefit in its own right, because they valued autonomy, but they also observed how the increased evidence that they were trusted made them take more interest in the job. Moreover, there was now much less waiting around for orders, guidance, spares or supplies. Already the pattern that is emerging begins more and more to resemble the characteristics of the autonomous work group. (Trist *et al.*, 1963)

Thirdly, 62 per cent of the men said that their work had become more interesting as a result of the changes. This percentage is substantially lower than of those who felt that working conditions had improved, which suggests that the enrichment of work actually done, and the tasks involved, had been more modest. This suggestion is supported by their explanation of why they felt the work had become more interesting, which indicates that the real meaning to them of the changes in task was that the work had become less boring rather than more interesting: less a source of deprivation rather than a source of positive gratification. The job was less tedious but remained inherently an uninteresting set of tasks or, as one man put it, 'It's not interesting to the point where you can enjoy it.'

There were further signs that as time went on the men became accustomed to the new methods of working. They were becoming the new routine and the injection of new interest was beginning to wear off. These signs lead us into our conclusions on job enrichment, where we can link the implications of our two case studies with the earlier material in Chapters One and Two.

Conclusions

Job enrichment and technological contraints

The first conclusion that we can draw is that there are powerful arguments for job enrichment on both economic and social grounds. While it is feasible in a large variety of jobs, there are, however, wide variations in the scope for practical application among different groups of workers in industry. The chief limitation on effective job enrichment for large sectors of industry is the constraints imposed by the primary technology employed in the process of production, which is in turn dictated by the present state of technological innovation. At the moment the general stage that we are going through in industry can by styled as one of sophisticated mechanization which imposes severe limits on the scope of workers' self expression but as automation increases so the scope for both viable organizational choice and the opportunity for designing job structures that permit real job interest, autonomy and responsibility will grow. Both these points can be illustrated by our case studies. As far as the petro-chemical workers were concerned, working under a continuous-process system where automation is at present most advanced, they already enjoyed relatively high levels of autonomy and opportunity to use and develop their abilities. It was relatively easy for the job to be enriched beyond this comparatively high starting point without management consciously striving to do so. The nylon spinners, however, started at a low level of intrinsic reward and it proved very difficult to raise the character of the job content to a level that was qualitatively different. It is perhaps useful here to distinguish between the constraints imposed on worker autonomy by systems of managerial control and those imposed by the technology itself. It was possible to change the style of management, reduce the number of supervisors and closeness of supervision, and delegate a range of decisions previously taken by supervision to the men themselves.

To moderate the control exercised over the men by the dictates of the method of production was far more difficult. Thus while the men experienced real benefits in terms of freedom from supervision, and through the heightened level of co-operation and work sharing within the work group, they did not experience the same degree of benefit in terms of changes in the actual tasks they had to do.

That their time was more fully occupied and that they did a greater variety of tasks meant that their day was less boring and time passed more quickly, but the tasks themselves remained undemanding and uninteresting.Moreover there were signs that as time passed the new methods of working became the new routine and the degree of enhanced interest declined.

While seeking to assess the implications of this type of change for the rest of industry realistically, we do not seek to deprecate its very real achievements,but merely to moderate any tendency to see job enrichment as something that could transform the position of manual workers. What does seem true is that while there is likely to be some scope for job enrichment in the large majority of jobs, the scope may be very limited at some stages in the development of technology. It is even more difficult to see any real opportunity in this type of production process for a continuing and progressive process of growth and development for industrial workers.

Job enrichment and collective advancement

The lack of scope for progressive development remains a major distinction between many blue-collar and white-collar jobs and a brief consideration of this distinction will provide a basis for making our second chief qualification about what can realistically be expected of job enrichment when applied to manual workers. First, the nature of many white-collar jobs is such as to provide greater scope for job enrichment even within the jobs that white-collar workers now do. Their jobs tend to provide more scope for organizational choice. They are not subject to the same constraints from the purely mechanical demands of the process of production. But secondly, and perhaps even more importantly, they tend very much more than the blue-collar workers to be able to look forward to the possibility of continuous and progressive growth throughout their working lives, although this is less true for women. The men, however, can expect a succession of different jobs, a succession that is progressively more challenging and demanding, that provides new interest and scope for achievement in mastering the new job and that requires training so that there is a continuous process of personal development and increasingly greater opportunities to use and develop abilities. In short, for the white-collar worker, the concept of a career as opposed to a job still has some meaning, even if at some levels it may be declining. Where it exists, however, it is a powerful force for job involvement and creates a strong link between the fortunes of the individual and those of the enterprise. His individual advancement is dependent upon his performance as rated by his superiors and as the enterprise grows and develops so do the opportunities for the career employee.

The general pattern for the blue-collar worker is very different. For him the probabilities are that he will continue to be a manual wage earner for the whole of his working life. His realistic expectation is that he will continue to do the job he is doing or a very similar level of job until he retires. While it may be possible to enrich the job he is doing, even substantially, it is not realistic to expect that it might be possible to create progressively more interesting, responsible, challenging and demanding jobs for him. Thus, in terms of the components of Herzberg's job enrichment package, the one element that is missing for the manual worker, and which it seems likely that it would be impossible to introduce in anything other than an artificial way, is scope for individual advancement. In terms of involvement in work and attitudes to management and trade unions this is the critical component. Given that the manual worker's realistic expectation is that he will remain in the same type of job that he is in at present and that his scope for individual advancement is limited or non-existent, then any hope that he has of advancement in his status and earnings lies in the advancement of the group of which he is a member. In short his economic and social advancement is linked inextricably to collective advancement, for it is only if the wage or salary grade to which he belongs receives an improvement in earnings, fringe benefits, status or conditions that he will progress.

Some of the implications of this are well illustrated by the attitudes of our group of petro-chemical workers to promotion in an industry where opportunities for personal advancement up to and including foreman level remain fairly good compared with the position of manual workers generally. There were in this case four grades of operator below the level of foreman, which provided a promotion structure up which men with knowledge and experience could progress. The men generally favoured movement up the seniority structure because it meant more interest, higher earnings and increased status. Where such advancement had been linked to their own performance and achievements they found it a personal source of gratification, as was illustrated by answers to Herzberg-type questioning. Yet in general they opposed promotion on 'merit' (or rather of management being allowed to select men for promotion on its definition of merit) and supported promotion on seniority with certain built-in safeguards such as union/management agreement that the man was up to the job. And they eschewed the opportunity for personal advancement that promotion on merit might give them because they perceived that ultimately their own interests were linked more to collective than to individual advancement. As such, if they permitted promotion on a managerial definition of merit, this would reduce their collective strength and their basis for collective action to protect and advance their interests. They argued that if management were allowed to select men unilaterally for promotion it would favour 'yes men' and 'blue-eyed boys' and penalize militants. This would divide the men, discourage militancy, reduce solidarity and weaken their bargaining strength with management in areas of conflict. Thus their perception of conflicts of interest, and their awareness that ultimately their own advancement was linked inextricably to that of the group of which they were members, led them to forgo opportunities for personal gratification in the interests of collective strength.

This once again exposes the limitations of the Herzberg approach, indicating that the response of workers to the intrinsic rewards of job content can be understood only in terms of the social and economic frameworks of job content. Here the requirements for effective collective advancement took precedence over apparently increased opportunity for individual advancement. In the same way the men's initial evaluations of the agreements were related to a perspective of collective advancement rather than to their own individual experience of rewards and deprivation on the job. It is true that, all other things being equal, men prefer activity to standing around idle half the day; interest to boredom; use of abilities rather than having to do routine, undemanding tasks. They are indeed often shocked by waste and inefficiency. But all other things are not equal and in particular are complicated by the social and economic relationships between management and men, especially the relationship between job content and remuneration and the strategies that men adopt to strengthen their bargaining position.

This does not mean, as is quite clear from our findings, that job content is unimportant or that job enrichment is not practicable or desirable. What it does mean is that as far as these types of manual workers are concerned, job enrichment has to be placed in a collective bargaining context and, as we have tried to demonstrate, management has to distinguish between the different attitudes, priorities and strategies that prevail in different contexts. It also means that job enrichment in blue-collar jobs is not going to change the fundamental relationship between management and labour in the way some hopeful managers have assumed, but rather that it will make for improvement within that fundamental relationship.

Indeed, rather than it being possible through job enrichment to transform the industrial worker into the traditional managerial ideal of a committed, loyal, staff worker, all the signs are that one trend narrowing the difference that we have distinguished between the job structure of manual and non-manual workers is bringing the relationship of non-manual workers with management closer to that of manual workers. The growth of the white-collar sector and the size of employment units within that sector, with the accompanying formalization of organization and procedures, has tended to bring about a situation in which more and more white-collar workers are finding themselves in the position where their advancement is more closely linked to their grade and group than it is to personal career achievement and progress. Thus they too are increasingly turning towards strategies for collective advancement through unionization.

Job enrichment and management structure

The third main conclusion emerging from our findings and reviews is that the importance of job enrichment for a particular group of workers must not be seen in isolation from the rest of the organization. What comes out clearly is that the type of reorganization we have been discussing has important implications for management style as a whole. This is demonstrated most directly by the effects it has upon supervision or first-line management. The one essential characteristic of any really effective change in the direction of job enrichment is the delegation of greater responsibility to individual workers and work groups, so that some shop-floor decision making passes from supervisors to the work group. But this immediately changes the position of the supervisor and there will be uncertainty for all at this level. This does not necessarily mean that fewer first-line managers or foremen will be needed or that their span of control will be increased but rather that the numbers at intermediary levels, such as assistant foremen, will be reduced or even eliminated. The jobs of those remaining will be very substantially changed. Indeed they may well feel that their last remaining vestige of status and responsibility has been stripped from them.

Industrial change has brought about a progressive impoverishment of the job of the first-line supervisor. As we described in Chapter Two, the development of specialist functions has meant that more and more of his traditional job has been whittled away until all that is often left is the day-to-day policing of the workers under his command. And now along comes job enrichment to divest him of this last remaining function. It is not enough to assume that being freed from the demands of detailed, direct and close supervision of the work and workforce will enable him for the first time to become an effective member of the management team and to contribute to a higher level of management planning and decision making. This is not a job that he has been trained to do and the new competence will not come spontaneously or automatically. Yet it is something that management has to ensure does come about through its reorganization of the management structure over the more autonomous work group, for nothing is more likely to jeopardize the results of the change than disgruntled supervisors reluctant to operate the new system of working even if they are capable of doing so. What is clearly required is that as much attention is paid to the jobs of supervisors, their interests, their responsibilities and job descriptions, and the training they will need to fulfil these, as is paid to the reorganization of shop-floor jobs. The key position of the first-line manager in the process of industrial change is something to which we shall refer repeatedly in our report.

Job enlargement and job rotation

In terms of improving the quality of jobs we have mainly focused on ways of increasing the levels of skill, ability, discretion and responsibility exercised by workers. We have recognized, however, that there are very many jobs where the scope for this is strictly limited. There remains the possibility that even within such jobs there may be some scope for injecting greater interest through job enlargement or rotation. It may be impossible to enrich jobs vertically, but possible to extend them to include a greater variety of tasks, although each task may not require greater skill ᴑor ability. Alternatively it may be possible to engender variety and renewed interest by moving workers around from one task to another. These are feasible, if palliative, alternatives. There are, however, two major considerations to be taken into account when considering their desirability.

The first of these is the danger of again regarding job content in isolation and not taking into account the impact that changes in job content have upon social relationships on the job and other sources of gratification or compensation. There is a tendency to assume that the relationship between task complexity or variety, job interest and job satisfaction represents a straight line: the more complex or varied a set of tasks are, the more interesting the job will be and the more satisfied the worker will be with the result. In practice this has been found not to be the case for, as far as very simple assembly jobs are concerned, the tasks are such that they allow the operator to perform them unthinkingly, automatically, even unconsciously. This frees the mind to day-dream or think about something distinct from the task being done, or alternatively to chat, gossip, joke and interact socially with other members of the work group – if noise, distance and relationship make this possible. There tends to come a point when the complexity of the tasks require full attention, making both fantasy and social interaction impossible, while the tasks themselves are still not sufficiently interesting or rewarding to compensate for the loss of social contact or day-dreams.

Similarly job rotation and enlargement may break up established work-group relationships, without substantially increasing the interest of the job. Indeed it may well be that management attempts to impose rotation or enlargement on the work group will achieve exactly the opposite of what management is setting out to do. Workers may see the attempts as moves towards closer supervision and more control over activity and task distribution. As we have been at pains to emphasize, one essential component of increased worker discretion in the job is less supervision. In practice, work groups and their members will, if given the opportunity, tend spontaneously in their informal social and task organization to make the work as interesting and palatable as they can. They adopt informal practices of job sharing and rotation among themselves and vary both pattern and pace of work within groups, to suit individual preferences and abilities to the extent that they are permitted to do so by supervision and the physical organization of the plant. What the work group cannot control unilaterally, of course, is the style and degree of supervision, the level of manning and the technical and physical layout of the plant. Management has to make the changes in these areas. We have seen in the second case, for instance, how critical are the numbers of supervisors and the closeness of the supervision, and the levels of manning, to the experience of autonomy, co-operation among work group members, and job interest, at work.

Thus, as far as job rotation and enlargement are concerned, management must create the conditions where this can naturally come about, through the style of supervision, the level of manning and the physical layout of the work area, rather than by imposing preconceived systems of rotation and enlargement on the work group. Though the intention may be to increase the workers' job interest and autonomy the effect is likely to reduce them because of closer supervision and loss of social satisfactions through the break-up of established group relationships. This again underlines the fact that work structuring is not an established technique which can be applied without consideration of the ideas and interests of the group members. While management may have ideas about desirable changes from previous experience and research, the details have to be worked out with the work group involved, and their ideas incorporated, if the results are to be effective.

Throughout this chapter, in seeking to place work structuring into perspective, we have been at pains to moderate any tendency to be over-enthusiastic about its scope and effects. We have emphasized the technological constraints. We have highlighted the importance of locating changes in job content in the framework of strong social and economic influences and have demonstrated how important it is to understand the variations in workers' priorities and attitudes towards management when seeking to restructure jobs and predict the likely benefits.

The aim, however, has been to encourage managements to approach work structuring realistically and constructively rather than to discourage them from considering or pursuing it. We have been able to demonstrate that, within most work situations, the system of organization adopted has an important impact for those operating it on the experience of work, job interest, relationships with work-mates and relationships with management; that adopting a form of organization which enriches the job increases job satisfaction, feelings of involvement and levels of effectiveness and provides a basis for a more constructive relationship between management and employees. We can safely conclude that both management and unions should increasingly examine the content of the jobs that people do in order to see how they might usefully be restructured. Both in the design and running of plant they need to pay much closer attention to the human implications of different alternatives rather than to engineering and financial considerations alone.

Section Two

Worker Involvement in Decision Making and Representation

4 Introduction

Our continuing theme throughout this book is that there are few changes more necessary for achieving industry's economic and social goals than greater worker involvement in decision making. As will be clear, we see no one single dramatic change, such as a change in ownership or in the composition of the industrial organization's governing body, that will automatically bring in a new era of industrial democracy overnight. Indeed we argue that such changes are in many ways irrelevant, that most of the barriers to effective worker involvement in decision making are independent of ownership and the composition of boards, and that the same types of changes need to be made regardless of ownership and control at the top. If there is one single change that we consider the most important this is the acceptance by management of the need for greater worker involvement and its taking the initiative in creating channels and institutions for involvement. But within that broad framework we see the need for the development of a number of different media at different levels. In Section One we looked at two specific ways of extending the worker's discretion, influence and control in his day-to-day tasks and activities at work through job enrichment and the development of such ideas as the autonomous work group. Control and autonomy at this level, we suggested, were those often most spontaneously sought by workers. Now, in Section Two, we look at ways of widening the employee's influence over events still further. And we do so not in any abstract, theoretical or idealistic way but rather by looking at the practical initiatives that some managements have taken in order to enable them to manage more effectively. In particular we examine total involvement programmes brought about by the need for major change; the adjustments in management style, philosophy and practice that these have necessitated; the reforms in institutions for representation that they have brought about, creating machinery for communication, involvement and joint decision making on a permanent basis; the extension of joint job regulation through integrating joint-consultative and collective-bargaining channels; and the development of the trade union as the chief channel of representation for employees. Indeed, although we see the need for a range and variety of different media for worker involvement at different levels, we argue that generally these should be developed within the over-all framework of joint management/union agreement and control. If there is one other common theme that runs through our analysis it is the need for greater devolution of decision making. This is essentially on the basis that if local management is not in a position to take independent decision, or is very restricted in the extent of its decision-making powers, then there is very little scope for worker involvement in decision making. Conversely, the nearer decisions are made to the place of work, the more potential there is for workers to exercise influence. Again, as we shall see, many managements have found that this makes good practical sense as well as increasing worker involvement.

In this introductory section we sketch in the chief developments that demand more worker involvement in decision making, and look at some sources of variation in different types of industrial organization that permit such involvement to take differing forms. We go on in subsequent chapters to examine in some detail the different media for involvement mentioned.

The case for worker involvement in decision making

The pressure for giving workers a greater say in decisions has come from three main sources. The first is the increasing acceptance by management of the simple, common sense proposition that people are more committed to aims, objectives or goals that they themselves have played a part in setting, than they are to those that are imposed upon them from above. To put it another way, no one is more in favour of a new idea than the man who first thought of it, from which it follows that if you want people to be strongly in favour of a new idea, the answer is to try and ensure that it comes from them. These simple propositions have been confirmed by a massive volume of research showing that employee participation in decision making can lead to heightened job satisfaction, improved performance and greater acceptance of change. The results of an enormous number of such research studies which support this conclusion, from Hawthorne (Roethlisberger and Dixon, 1964), onwards, have been exhaustively reviewed and summarized by Blumberg who concludes, 'There is hardly a study in the entire literature which fails to demonstrate that satisfaction in work is enhanced or that other generally acknowledged beneficial consequences accrue from a genuine increase in workers' decision making power'. (Blumberg, 1968)

Blumberg uses this conclusion to make a powerful plea for greater industrial democracy as the only generally applicable means of overcoming alienation in work. And indeed it is the demand for just that which provides the second chief source of pressure for heightened worker influence over decisions. In this context the argument goes that people's jobs and work are perhaps the most important sectors of their lives. A man spends half his adult waking life at work. His job is his chief source of income and self-respect and determines both his status in the community and his standard of life. The nature of his work can be shown to have a critical influence on his style and quality of life, his pattern of consumption, spare time and leisure activities. If democracy is to have any real meaning, it is suggested, then it should be extended to this critical area of people's lives. In this way the pressure for industrial democracy, and for the greater control of employees over decisions that directly affect what is the core of their lives, can be seen to both mirror and reinforce one of the most powerful social movements, nationally and internationally, of the 1960s: the demand of those who are in subordinate positions in power relationships in society, be they religious or racial minorities, women, the poor or the young, or employees, for greater influence in shaping their destinies. As such, this second source of pressure for involvement has its origins in social values rather than the practical need to increase communal wealth by making the process of manufacture, distribution and exchange more efficient.

Nevertheless it clearly has practical implications for management and indicates the third chief source of pressure for increasing the area of employee involvement. This is indeed the most practical argument of all: that unless industry can make its policies and practices consistent with social values outside industry, unless its managers can accommodate these powerful social movements, not only will industry be less efficient than it otherwise might be, but ultimately management will lose control and be unable to manage at all and will increasingly be able to retain or recover control or power only by sharing it. It will have to give more power to employees and their representatives. The idea that more power should be given, for instance, to trade unions as employees' representatives may at first seem odd to many managers, who are sometimes inclined to believe that most of our industrial problems − resistance to change, restrictive practices, wage-push inflation − are the result of the fact that many unions have too much power already. And it is true that unions in some sectors of the economy do have a great deal of bargaining power. But the nature of this power is, often as a direct result of the role that they are allotted by management, wholly the power to obstruct and oppose. As we shall see through some of the examples in this section, where unions are given the opportunity to play a constructive, creative role they can be a powerful force for facilitating change rather than obstructing it. Similarly, so much of pathological industrial behaviour, from managements' point of view, and that of the efficiency of the enterprise, such as restrictive practices and restriction of output,* can be directly interpreted as symptoms of workers' needs to exercise some control over their immediate work situation. Equally, in a situation where employees in the most menial of jobs exercise considerable discretion, and work groups substantial power, to try to overcome this by exercising greater and tighter control is self-defeating and produces a vicious circle. In fact the constructive way to deal with this is by giving employees greater discretion, and work groups greater autonomy, so that they have an opportunity to exercise greater control over the job, but in a way that serves efficiency goals rather than obstructs them. This was exactly the intention in the case of many of the examples we have described in Section One.

This highlights again, however, how the greatest spontaneous demand for control comes from the desire for more discretion and

---

* The widely observed tendency for groups of workers employed under PBR schemes to set standards of performance or output that are below what they could achieve, and for the group members to conform to those standards.

autonomy on the job. It is for this reason we have emphasized how the starting point for greater involvement of the employee lies in the tasks he does, the way these are organized and his relationship with his immediate boss. If we were dealing with a perfectly stable situation then it might be that changes at this level would not only be among the most important but might also be sufficient. But far from being in a stable situation we are in a rapidly changing one. Industry needs to change in order to reform outdated practices, procedures and systems of organization and remuneration; and it needs to change to accommodate technological and product innovation. It is this need for change that creates the second area where worker involvement is of crucial importance, for it is the demand to have a say in the form of changes that affects workers directly and critically and represents the other most spontaneously expressed desire for involvement.

It is one means for accommodating this demand, through total involvement change programmes, that we discuss in Chapter Five. But we shall see that, although it is in circumstances of major change that a high level of involvement is often most relevant, valuable and most spontaneously sought after, once management has set its foot on this road, inevitably and necessarily other consequences result, including, as we shall show, the need for machinery for involvement and joint regulation on a permanent basis, usually through the medium of the trade union.

Sources of variation in forms of involvement

But before going on to develop this general theme there are two points that we have to clarify: the one refers to our own value position and the other to the way in which different styles and approaches are appropriate to different circumstances. First, as will have become clear from our introduction, the impetus for greater employee involvement in decision making derives from both practical considerations and social values. On the one hand, it is argued that greater employee involvement leads to the smoother and more effective running of enterprises, and may even become essential if they are to run at all. On the other hand, it is argued that the lack of involvement is a denial of democratic freedom, regardless, by implication at least, of the effects on the economic performance of the enterprise.

Our own position on this is clear. We find that there is impressive evidence that greater involvement does lead to a healthier enterprise and will increasingly become necessary if change is to be accepted and growth achieved. But equally we recognize that all the media for involvement we describe here will not be feasible or appropriate under all circumstances. At the same time we share the desire for greater involvement based on social values and would argue that, just as in the case of job enrichment, where there are alternative methods of managing, it is up to those who advocate or practice authoritarian methods to demonstrate that the alternative is so economically damaging as to be wholly unrealistic, rather than the other way round.

Secondly, as we made clear in Section One, there are important variations in what is appropriate to different types of workplace with regard to most, if not all, management practices. One of the most important sources of variation in terms of the most appropriate form of worker involvement in decision making can be illustrated by further reference to the findings of the two case studies that we quoted there. These showed how workers' attitudes to management, their motivations and their priorities in what they sought from the job varied at different points in time, and in different contexts. The agreements were initially viewed with strong reservations or even outright hostility and were introduced only after hard bargaining over the men's increase in earnings in relation to the increased workload they would have to carry. But subsequently they were welcomed more for the increased intrinsic rewards that they brought about than for the increases in earnings and fringe benefits.

Within this change in attitude can be identified the two main and distinct contexts where apparently contradictory but psychologically viable images of the relationship between management and worker prevailed. On the one hand was the work situation where what was important was, first, the content of jobs, the scope that they provided for interest and the use and development of abilities and, secondly, the quality of social relationships with work-mates and management in day-to-day contact on the job. Here attitudes to management were more characterized by the teamwork concept. On the other hand was the negotiating context where what was important to workers was their share of the wealth generated by the enterprise. So what they were interested in here was maximizing their earnings and fringe benefits at the same time as protecting their long-term interests by preserving their power and fulfilling felt obligations to a wider community of industrial workers. In this context attitudes to management were characterized more by an awareness of conflict and divergence of interests. This difference between attitudes to management in different contexts can be further illustrated by the men's answers to two other questions in the petro-chemical case.

They were asked whether they thought the firm could afford to pay them more without harming its own prospects for the future, and whether they felt they were under pressure from management in carrying out their work. Every respondent was convinced that the firm could afford to pay more. But at the same time there was virtually unanimous agreement that they were under no pressure in carrying out their work and were generally left to carry on with the job in their own way without interference. Here again there was the pattern of differing interests with regard to the distribution of the wealth generated by the enterprise, but more common interests in the carrying out of the work. This distinction was succinctly summed up by the comment, 'On the job we work as a team. When it comes to money we're on different sides'. It is not quite as simple as that but this does highlight a distinction often made. Of course these findings were derived from men working under continuous-process technology, and the distinctions here will by no means be as clear-cut in all industries and workplaces. But what we believe is more generally true is the ways in which employees identified both common and divergent interests and how motivation or job priorities varied from context to context.

Unfortunately there has been a tendency among different groups of researchers who have sought to study industrial behaviour, motivation and employee relations, and through this study to identify means of improving worker effectiveness and labour relations, to focus upon just one of these contexts to the neglect of the other. Thus one approach, which could be loosely termed the 'human relations' or socio-psychological approach, such as that adopted by Herzberg, Argyris, (1964) McGregor, (1966) and Likert, (1961) has focused very much upon attitudes, motivations and satisfactions in the workplace, in day-to-day activities and relationships on the job. This type of approach demonstrated the importance of job content, intrinsic interest, the quality of relationships with the immediate superior and within the work group as important determinants of involvement, satisfaction and attitudes. And they have suggested job enrichment, participative styles of management, more appropriate work-group organization and improved communication and consultation as means of improving employing effectiveness. But often when the manager is presented with such conclusions — that, for instance, suggest to him that the worker is primarily interested in greater scope for achievement through the use and development of abilities, greater intrinsic interest and responsibility, opportunities for advancement and the exercise of responsibility — he finds that it does not correspond to his experience. Indeed, on the contrary, his experience suggests strongly that workers are primarily interested in money and resisting and opposing management as far as they can. But this is because he tends to talk to workers about their jobs in only one set of contexts: when he is negotiating change and new rates; or when they are taking or leaving a job. And it is in these contexts that workers are most interested in earnings and most aware of conflict. Thus management gets a distorted view of attitudes and priorities and then generalizes the attitudes and motivations expressed, assumes that they represent the full picture and dismisses the socio-psychological approaches as irrelevant, academic nonsense or idealistic, when in fact they are relevant but to quite different contexts.

Alternatively, different types of manager take a quite contrary view. They enthusiastically embrace the 'human relations' findings and see them as a means of breaking out of the problem caused by conflict. They see the findings as a basis for establishing a new style of management that will reduce or eliminate differences of interest. They conclude that if they can bring about job enrichment and participative, supportive styles of supervision that give full regard to the individual, if they can improve communication and consultation, then they will increase job satisfaction, identification with management and the enterprise. They will overcome any feelings of 'us and them' and introduce a new era of harmony by weaning workers away from attachments to trade unions which, they feel, foment and exacerbate conflict. In this way any worker need or demand for involvement in decision making will be satisfied by management taking the initiative to introduce job enrichment, consultative styles of supervision and formal joint consultation. We have seen in Section One the weaknesses in this general argument as far as job enrichment is concerned. And indeed this strategy is not generally applicable because, like the 'socio-psychological' approaches themselves from which it derives, it is limited and partial. It is based on an analysis of just one of the contexts that we have identified and ignores both the differences in power enjoyed by management and labour and the potential, perceived and real differences of interest between different parties to the enterprise and thus the importance of collective bargaining.

The alternative general approach to the study of industrial behaviour and employee relations, however, which includes the orientations of both institutional industrial relations and labour economics, has done the opposite. It has focused very much on the negotiating context and ways of regulating or resolving the conflicts between management and labour, and means of linking the economic attachment of the employee to his work, to his performance also. Thus this approach has suggested improved procedures and institutions for collective bargaining and negotiation, comprehensive plant agreements, productivity agreements, creative bargaining for change, quicker and more effective grievance and arbitration procedures, and more rational, equitable systems of payment less prone to generate disputes, as the means of regulating potential sources of overt conflict and improving employee relations.

As the case studies we have quoted amply illustrate, it is when attention is focused on both contexts with clear awareness of the different priorities and attitudes characteristic of them, that the most effective progress can be made. At the same time, although we have argued that the recognition of both common interests and conflicts of interest, and a mixture of different priorities varying according to context, are typical of most workers in most workplaces, we also recognize that there is a spectrum. Some workplaces and workers are generally characterized by a conflict, as opposed to a common interest, image of the management/employee relationship, and equally some are more characterized by a concern in all circumstances for extrinsic rewards or earnings than for intrinsic rewards or job satisfaction.

At one end of the spectrum there will be workplaces where relationships are in continuous and permanent conflict and no common interests perceived. At the other end there will be those where there is at least the appearance of harmony and acceptance by workpeople that their best interests are directly in line with those of management.

There has been a tendency for those writers and researchers on industrial behaviour who have pursued the alternative approaches that we have identified to seek or be able to gain access to those workplaces where their approach is more appropriate. Consequently and not surprisingly they have been able to confirm their basic assumptions. Thus ever since Hawthorne there has been a tendency for the classical 'human relations' studies to be carried out in workplaces with a paternalistic management which attaches high importance to its responsibilities towards employees; where there is a non-unionized labour force content to leave management to manage as best it sees fit, not seeking to restrict management's discretion or resist change in any organized or collective manner as opposed to such individual action as is indicated by turnover, absenteeism and sickness rates or individual output. Moreover such workplaces have often been set in a semi-rural environment with none of the history of mass unemployment, prolonged, bitter battles with employers for union recognition and minimum rights which are characteristic of the industrial working class in traditional industrial areas.

Equally, at the other end of the spectrum, we have workplaces where perception of conflict is so high and suspicions of management's motives and strategies so great that managers are not permitted direct access to the workforce or allowed to speak to employees individually. In this type of situation it is clear that a start on the improvement of employee relations can be made only at the level of formal collective bargaining rather than at the level of interpersonal relationships between management and employees.

We are working on the basis that the large proportion of workplaces lie between these two poles, and our analysis in this section of the means of giving employees more say over their affairs at work points to the conclusion that for this proportion, these means tend inexorably to lead to the recognition of the trade union as the chief medium for representing employees.

At the same time, given that there is a spectrum, it is hardly surprising if there are some companies which have achieved a relatively high level of employee involvement and participation through alternative means, without recognizing trade unions at all. Such companies have tended to be successful family businesses which have attached a high priority to their responsibilities towards employees and have taken the view that because employees' interests are so effectively protected and furthered, and because the voice of employees is so quickly heard and heeded within the framework of the existing management philosophy, style and machinery, then a third party to promote the interests and channel the voice of employees is neither necessary to employees nor desired by them.

Such a management style and philosophy as expressed, for instance, in Marks & Spencer and IBM, takes the following form. First, the level of salaries and wages paid, conditions of employment provided and amenities and physical working conditions furnished are markedly better than those normal elsewhere. Secondly, there is a highly trained and highly capable management team fully schooled in human relations techniques. Management is organized in such a way that each manager has a relatively small span of control and a relatively high level of autonomy and discretion in recruiting, employing and rewarding his work team, with no layer or level of supervision intervening between the manager and those under his command, so that he is able to develop a detailed personal knowledge of the strengths, weaknesses and personal characteristics of each individual under his command and develop a personal relationship with him. Thirdly, responsibility is delegated as far down the hierarchy as is feasible and job enrichment is practised in order to increase autonomy and control at the workplace. Fourthly, there are well developed, joint-consultative procedures and, fifthly, there is a liberal use of employee-attitude surveys, conducted at frequent and regular intervals to identify areas of discontent and dissatisfaction and, through feed-back to the joint-consultative machinery and work teams, to modify practices in line with findings.

Thus, through job enrichment, supportive, participative styles of management, joint-consultation and attitude surveys, the freedom of the employee and the expression of his ideas, interests and wishes are extended as far as is consistent with management retaining power, control and the right to take decisions unilaterally. This approach seems to have succeeded, where it has been developed, in achieving a high level of performance from employees, together usually with substantial commitment to the enterprise. It is worth again underlining, however, some of the characteristics of the organizations and their environments where it has succeeded.

They tend, first, as already mentioned, to be family firms inspired by the personal drive and philosophy of the family ownership, which has managed to imprint this philosophy upon professional managers, dedicated to the ideas of the enterprise and its success. Secondly, they have enjoyed a very favourable and growing market for the enterprises' products and have consequently enjoyed a pervasive atmosphere of success, growth and achievement. This degree of growth has enabled financial rewards to match the human relations rewards within the organization. It has also contributed to the development of a distinctive identity and image outside the enterprise; this, together with the high rewards furnished on virtually all job dimensions, has meant that there has been a strong demand for jobs in the enterprise – coming particularly from those who are favourably disposed to the philosophy of the organization – and, very importantly, that it has been possible to select applicants whose attitudes and characteristics are most consistent with those of the enterprise. Thirdly, the growth and development has been internal and self-sufficient, rather than brought about by amalgamations and mergers. This has enabled management to keep the house philosophy, policies and practices pure, consistently selecting and socializing new recruits to fit in with them, rather than having large alien bodies introduced into the organization at different points in time, whose policies and practices would have to be radically changed to bring them into line with those of the parent body.

Much of industry, however, does not find itself in this situation. It does not have such a favourable market and growth. It does not have an uninterrupted history of steady success and development. It does not have a top management attaching a high priority to employees' interests nor a highly professional middle management which fully embraces and shares the values of top management.It does not have a consistent philosophy and set of policies and practices throughout the organization. And it does not have a workforce which is content to accept either unilateral management decision making, or the idea that because of its professional or technical expertise and profound concern for employees' interests, every decision that management takes is unchallengeable and in the best interests of all employees.

On the contrary management finds itself in a situation, not where it has to maintain and develop a good system, but rather where it must change and where that change will be painful. And painful change means conflict. It must close plants and make others more efficient, and to do so it must make people and skills redundant. It must reorganize and rationalize and, in this process of reorganizing vast numbers of people in large units, it is forced to deal with people on many issues as aggregates or collectivities rather than as individuals. And it can initiate and implement this process of change only with an at least minimum level of consent from employees. This is a daunting task and one in which participative styles of management, joint consultation and attitude surveys are unlikely on their own to prove fully effective. We believe that a great degree of employee involvement in decision making can facilitate this process of change and in the rest of this section we illustrate both why this is so and how it can work. But while starting out from a point quite consistent with the participative managerial, socio-psychological approach we end up way beyond it.

5 Total involvement exercises

One area in which the value of greater employee involvement in decision making is firmly established as appropriate, feasible, and effective is, as we indicated in Chapter Four, the facilitating of major change. One of the earliest experimental demonstrations of this was the classic Coch and French study of resistance to change among machinists in a clothing factory. (Coch and French, 1948) The chief problem had been that when methods were changed, operators took much longer than was necessary to learn the new methods, and this long learning period was accompanied by a great deal of hostility towards supervision and management. An experiment was set up in which one group changed practices in the normal way, a second elected representatives who were concerned with discussing the design of the changes, and in a third all members of the group were involved in discussing the changes. Results showed that the greater the involvement, the shorter was the learning period following the introduction of the changes and the less was the hostility expressed towards management and supervision. It should be borne in mind that, like so many of the great socio-pysychological, industrial experiments, this was carried out in a non-unionized firm in a semi-rural, light industrial area. It also referred to an all-female labour force.

But the examples of recent total involvement exercises for change in British industry that took a similar approach were all carried through in fully unionized firms, in industrial areas with all-male workforces. They demonstrate equally well the creative force for change represented by high worker involvement in decision making; but they also demonstrate how in these types of situation the involvement cannot be on a purely consultative basis – where management can accept or reject workers' ideas as it sees fit – but rather that it has to be on a joint-regulative basis within which agreement has to be reached with workers through their representatives, and differing ideas and interests have to be reconciled, accommodated and resolved before effective change is brought about. Equally, half of the equation necessary to bring this about was the consideration of the workers' share of the economic benefits brought about by change.

Major industrial change in which high worker involvement in decision making is necessary if it is to be designed, implemented and operated effectively tends to be of two main types. The first is the reform of existing and out-of-date practice and procedures, such as working methods, the organization of tasks and jobs, and systems of pay based on industrial and technological forms that no longer exist. The second is the introduction of new plant that requires different methods of working. Most of the examples we have relate to the reform of out-of-date systems, though we believe that the principles on which they were based are equally appropriate to the facilitation of technological innovation.

The ICI Gloucester case

The first of these is the ICI Gloucester case, the job enrichment aspects of which we considered in Chapter Three. This was one of the three trial sites for the ICI Weekly Staff Agreement programme before it was generally implemented throughout the company. Essentially the change programme sought three chief objectives. First, it set out to reorganize working practices in a way that would on the one hand give workers greater responsibility, freedom from supervision and the chance to use and develop their abilities more fully, and on the other give management much more efficient utilization of manpower. Secondly, it sought to introduce a national, job-evaluation system that would simplify and rationalize differentials between different groups of workers. And, thirdly, it proposed to reform the system of payment by doing away with an outdated, payment-by-results scheme and introducing stable, weekly salaries paid for the new workloads and methods of working established by work study and agreement. Thus it was designed to bring substantial savings in labour costs and recognized that workers should have a share of those savings, and would be unlikely to accept the changes unless they did have. The basis of the change programme, then, was the agreeing of change beneficial to all parties, with the financial benefits being shared in an agreed way. Essentially it was a productivity agreement although, considering the disrepute into which the term 'productivity bargaining' has sunk, it is not surprising that ICI are disposed to think of it as 'much more than a productivity agreement'. For reasons set out at the end of this chapter we are disposed to think of it as representing the best type of productivity bargaining or, more exactly, creative bargaining for change.

We quote the Gloucester case because it has been the most extensively researched of all the ICI WSA applications, although the procedure adopted for introducing the changes was subsequently employed with modifications and with varying degrees of success (some of the reasons for which we pick up in the next chapter) across the company. The procedure had three main facets. First, there were shop-floor discussion groups in which the workers themselves discussed and proposed changes. Secondly, a joint management/union working party, composed of shop stewards, line management and work-engineering management, was set up to evaluate and co-ordinate the ideas coming through from the groups. And, thirdly, a joint union/management negotiating body was established to agree ultimately the changes worked out through the groups and the working party.

Management saw the shop-floor discussion groups as the key to the whole programme; all workers took part in at least one at some stage and many took part in more. They were led by supervisors, with shop stewards present, and set out to explain and discuss the changes proposed by management within the national framework agreement, as well as to discuss with workers the way they worked, the way their work was organized and any changes that might make their work more effective as well as more rewarding.

The discussion group is well established as an effective medium for communication, especially for two-way communication and for communicating information that is designed to change attitudes. It provides a situation in which ideas can be questioned, discussed, challenged and criticized freely and openly. It is a context in which it is recognized that the communication of information is not a mechanical process, that those to whom it is being directed have to interpret information before it becomes meaningful, and that this process of interpretation is often a social process. But, to be successful, such discussion groups need skilled leadership. They need group leaders who are adept at encouraging and allowing others to express their views, who draw out the quiet and the timid, who create an atmosphere in which any view however critical and challenging can be expressed, and who feel their way to a consensus rather than impose their own preconceived ideas on the group. ICI Gloucester were fortunate in having very good supervisors. Each had received twelve months' training, mostly on the job, after selection, before being appointed a supervisor. In addition, they received special training for this exercise including training in group-discussion leadership. Indeed it was estimated that in total about 40 man years were spent on training for the exercise, including management training, supervisor training, shop-steward training and operator training.

The way in which both supervisors and shop stewards were deeply involved in these groups was a very important feature of the whole programme. Although the groups were only one part of the over-all plan they were perhaps the most original and particularly pertinent to our theme in this section. It is therefore useful to look at how their effects and effectiveness were evaluated by the main parties: management and the men themselves.

One conclusion that can confidently be drawn is that on management's evaluation they were highly successful for three reasons.

First, the level of involvement and participation that managers observed was very high and the quality of the comment and suggestions for change produced, equally high. The men's special knowledge of the work and their unique perspective enabled them to identify sources of waste work, both in the way they operated and in the way their work was controlled, which only they could be aware of. It has to be borne in mind that management was satisfied that it had gone about as far as it could by conventional methods of achieving greater efficiency through the use of work study, O & M, the computer scheduling of work and a highly trained supervisory force. As a result of this, it had already been able to achieve levels of manning that were as good as, or better than, at any other similar plant in the UK, as had been established by comparative manning reviews. It followed from this that, if further substantial savings were to be made, they could be achieved only by alternative means. And the chief means that the management saw was the harnessing of the special knowledge and capabilities of the workforce to greater effect by getting them to help in devising and operating a new system of working which was dependent upon substituting self-control and self-regulation for the very much more expensive, and, as it turned out, less effective control by supervisors and by planning, quality, and work-control specialists. But management also rapidly became aware that such a new system of working could not be imposed on the workforce, could not even be designed independently of the workforce, and that in fact, in essence, it must come through the workforce. Thus in management's view it was only by the involvement of the workforce through the discussion groups that the productivity advances were made possible.

The second main benefit that the management saw in the discussion was that the changes were hammered out and discussed in a positive, co-operative spirit. Instead of management putting up proposals to be shot down by workers' representatives in formal negotiation, both parties were making suggestions and evaluating them reciprocally. Formal negotiations were kept to a minimum and indeed were virtually confined to the initial acceptance of the principle of applying the national agreement, and the eventual formal acceptance of the details that had been hammered out by the discussion groups and working parties in a session that lasted about half an hour.

The third chief benefit that management observed was the speed and smoothness with which the changes agreed were subsequently implemented after the details had been formally accepted. The changes involved a fundamental change in both the organization and methods of working, and made substantial new demands on workers. Yet because they had been so fully prepared by the discussion groups, the new system was introduced virtually overnight with no apparent difficulty or disturbance.

It should be emphasized here that though we are reporting management's view of the effects and effectiveness of the groups, it is quite consistent with the other information collected. First, there are two hard facts which cannot be discounted. The management started from a position of relatively high efficiency and yet were able to reduce the labour force (total 2,220) by 25 per cent as a result of the exercise. Secondly, the interviews with the men showed that they had clearly found the groups interesting and rewarding, and management responsive to their ideas and suggestions. Sixty-two per cent said that they thought the discussions had had a 'large' (28 per cent) or 'fair' (34 per cent) amount of influence on the form or detail of the changes that were introduced. Twenty-three per cent thought they had little or no influence. (Cotgrove, Dunham and Vanplew, 1971) Moreover the amount of influence attributed to the groups rose consistently with the number of groups attended, until of the men who had attended four or more discussions (17 men in the sample of 60), 88 per cent attributed a 'large' or 'fair' amount of influence to them. Although here it cannot be ruled out that the selection or self-selection of group members affects these responses, it does mean that those men who had been heavily involved in the groups felt that they had contributed substantially to the change.

In view of the way in which management conceived of the discussion groups – partly as a medium for enabling workers to see the benefit that they would gain from the changes in terms of increased job satisfaction and job interest – it is interesting to recall how they evaluated the changes both before these were implemented and afterwards. As we reported in Chapter Three, despite all the beneficial effects of the groups and the way that job interest featured in these, it was the promise of higher earnings that was the chief, if not the only, attraction of the changes before they were implemented, although the reasons for approving the new system, once operating, were much wider. This does not imply that the promise of higher earnings would have been sufficient on its own. Indeed we looked at another case in a similar nylon-spinning plant within a different company where they had tried to get similar changes within a conventional productivity agreement and, despite the fact that the increases in earnings were quite as high as those offered at Gloucester, management got nowhere. There may of course have been reasons, other than the difference in the level of involvement of workers and shop stewards in the design of the changes, why this should have occurred. But this does illustrate that the offer of increased earnings is often not in itself enough to facilitate smooth change; and together with our other information on their effects, it suggests that the involvement groups played a unique and indispensable part in the way the changes were developed, accepted and, particularly, implemented so smoothly and quickly. Nevertheless it is still worth emphasizing that this was possible only in a context where the savings brought about by the changes were shared in a way that the employees perceived as equitable, and where the workers were directly rewarded for their participation. There is a major difference between this type of exercise and the classic, socio-psychological, Coch and French experiment where involvement in the design of change was enough, alone, to ensure its ready and smooth acceptance, without any collective bargaining framework and without any direct sharing of the savings from the changes.

Other examples of involvement for change

In highlighting the success of the Gloucester case study there is a danger that this might be seen as something unique, brought about by a particularly inspired management or made possible by certain peculiar characteristics of the workforce. In fact the types of procedure adopted here, the types of change brought about and the greater worker involvement in decision making that they required and introduced, have grown increasingly more common in British industry in the 1960s. The same general approach was used when WSA was extended to the rest of ICI. Here, it is true, there was a pattern of variable success, but most of the company now operates the agreement and the large majority of applications have at least broken even in financial terms. At the same time, in management's view, they have brought about important structural changes in systems of representation and involvement, styles of management, and systems of payment, all of which provide a firm basis for constructive development and stable working relationships in the future.

But these developments have by no means been confined to ICI. They have been widely paralleled elsewhere. In some instances they have been more radical in so far as the one traditional feature of the ICI change programme was that it was based on a framework initially worked out and agreed at the centre. And it was only after and within this centralized framework that management started to build from the bottom, the point of change, upwards. Again we discuss some of the implications of this later. Here it is sufficient to say that some managements have taken the more daring (and those that see the paramount need for retaining over-all consistency and control at the top, might think dangerous) step of doing away with centralized company bargaining completely.

One such company that we looked at is Imperial Metal Industries

(IMI). Management there took the view that if constructive change were to be brought about, if management and workers were to make agreements appropriate to their circumstances, which were meaningful and would stick, then they had to be built from the bottom up by local plant management and their workers. They accepted that, although some of the agreements might look less than ideal from the centre, the more important consideration was that local plant management and workers should feel that they were *their* agreements. Then both parties would want to make them work, because they identified with something that they had devised, agreed and implemented themselves. The personal commitment and involvement in a unique plant agreement was likely to bring about a longer-lasting improvement in labour relations than something imposed or even suggested from the top.

Thus on one site employing some 10,000 workers, central bargaining ceased and plant management were left to work out their own salvation: to diagnose their problems, identify the means of resolving them, thrash out, agree and implement their own agreements. In many cases the problems were the same as those faced by ICI: the inefficient use of manpower, outdated payment systems and a confused and irrational distribution of differentials in earnings. And in many cases plant management came to similar conclusions about the need for reform and the ways this could be brought about. They too set up shop-floor discussion groups, joint working parties and joint-union negotiating bodies.

But here the similarity ends. Often there would be two plants working side by side employing different consultants, introducing different systems of job evaluation and different systems of payment, one an MDW scheme, another a production-based bonus scheme. It is important to underline that, although there were a number of different plants on the same site and decision making was fully decentralized to plant management, the plants were not integrated and interdependent. Each tended to be self-sufficient in being responsible for the total process in making a certain product or range of products. Moreover the complete decentralization did not mean that all site co-ordination was lost. Indeed top management argued that there was even more effective site co-ordination. Now that plant managers had the full responsibility for agreements operating in their plants and for the earnings of their workers, they were more concerned than ever to co-ordinate with other plant managers to ensure that different plants did not move too far out of line, because they had to bear the full brunt and carry the full responsibility for any undesirable effects of anomalies. Previously they had left it to centralized management to draw up agreements and ensure the maintenance of comparability and had been less interested in or committed to maintaining agreements and ensuring consistency. They were still aided it is true by a Works Employee Relations Manager, whose job was to help in the maintenance of consistency, but the value that plant managements had come to place upon their discretion and independence ensured that they retained the decision making function with regard to their own plants.

How far this type of development is generally applicable will clearly depend very much upon the degree of interdependence of plants in a large site, as well as all the other sources of variation we have cited. Equally it is unquestionably dependent on having strong, competent and confident, plant managers as well as a courageous top management. But where it has been applied it can be seen to take the process of worker involvement in decision making one stage further. The process of decentralization of decision making ensured that there were more decisions being taken at their level for employees to have an influence on. Shop-floor discussions, joint working parties and a joint union negotiating body were provided through which they could have an influence.

The common characteristics of change programmes

These same media for involvement have also been applied in the British Oxygen, English China Clays and BP Plastics change programmes. The common characteristics have been first the getting of as much discussion as possible on the shop floor with the workers who are going to operate the changes and whose job descriptions and work loads are going to change. This has sometimes been through the medium of formal discussion groups or on a much more informal basis.

All this does not of course mean that management can set up discussion groups and leave the workers to design a complete new organization. Management will, as it did in each case we looked at, have clear general ideas about the directions in which it wants to change and move. It used the discussions to test these ideas, to learn and to modify the ideas. It recognized that an imposed decision was less likely to be effective in practice, even if it was acceptable at all, than a discussed and agreed one.

Joint working parties were brought in through which the details of the changes were thrashed out in a joint problem-solving way. This required negotiation rather than consultation because the aim was to reach agreement. But agreement was reached through persuasion, through seeking new facts and alternative solutions to resolve differences, rather than through horse trading or compromise. A nice example of this is provided by the BP Barry case. Here the stage was reached where craft unions were strongly resisting the new job descriptions being worked out for general workers, as infringing their trade rights. They were therefore invited to draft what they would consider to be the proper job descriptions for general workers. They subsequently analysed the job and drew up their draft and this became acceptable as the basis for discussion and ultimately formed the main part of the general workers' new job descriptions. This is the imaginative way of resolving conflict that has been pioneered in such programmes.

The programmes have also tended to lead to completely new institutions, particularly negotiations with all unions represented on a site within a single, joint body rather than separate, sectional bargaining. To these we refer again later and in the next chapter.

The relevance and lessons of productivity bargaining

But, fourthly, it is worth referring to another common characteristic of these innovations in employee relations. They were all productivity agreements. The term 'productivity bargaining' has become so widely used, misused and abused that it is now hardly possible to use it without evoking howls of derision. Indeed there is increasing acceptance that the idea is 'dead'. In fact productivity bargaining was one of the most important innovations in British labour relations in the early 1960s. It achieved initial prominence in public discussion through the publication of Allan Flanders's account of the Esso 'blue book' at Fawley, when indeed he coined the term. (Flanders, 1964) But the practice received its real impetus from the last Labour Government's incomes policy, which under its productivity criteria allowed increases above the norm for the acceptance of changes in working practice that gave rise to higher labour productivity. But as well as bringing about the period of greatest activity in prductivity bargaining this also signed its death warrant. Such agreements became castigated as fraudulent shams in which management and workers conspired to enable the workers to get an increase regardless of the provision of the incomes policy. They were mocked as involving such petty practices as the buying out of tea breaks. They evoked horror at the alleged immorality in the buying out of restrictive practices. And they became firmly associated with the concept of a statutory incomes policy and so have shared the general disillusionment with such a policy. In fact judgements of this kind are a travesty of the best types of productivity agreement such as those we have referred to here, many of which themselves owed a great deal to the incomes policy. Indeed not only do these jibes seriously misrepresent the best types of agreement, but also, as our own studies show, they seriously understate the value and achievements of the general standard of agreements made under the productivity criterion of incomes policy. (Daniel, 1970)

Our analysis suggests that although we may cease to use the term productivity agreement, which was always a misleading and unfortunate one, and may never see another agreement bearing that title, there are certain ideas, principles and practices in the best types of productivity agreement that will have an enduring value for the management of change and the fostering of greater worker involvement in decision making. In fact many of these ideas were only implicit in much of what diferent managements were doing. They often did not spell them out and were even not fully aware of them. They were practical men concerned with the practical problems of bringing about change. But their practices can be seen to have been based on assumptions that were quite new in labour relations.

Essentially, productivity bargaining was the bringing about of changes through negotiation, at the same time as negotiating the share of the benefits of change that should go to the different parties. In practice this has meant the share that should go to the employer and the groups of workers involved. The National Board for Prices and Incomes (NBPI), through its productivity criterion, tried to establish the right of a third party, the community at large through the consumer, to a share of the savings. But we found no case in our studies where this principle was explicitly followed.

The changes that employers have sought to bring about through this type of agreement include reductions in excessive overtime, unnecessary but established and expected as of right to bolster low basic earnings; the changing of working practices, organization and job description between both different groups of craft workers on the one hand, and craft and general workers on the other, to make these more appropriate to the needs of production and the technology, thereby often increasing individual and group workloads and decreasing levels of manning; and the reform of systems of payment, to place differentials on a rational basis through job evaluation and thus do away with a multitude of largely meaningless premia for different kinds of performance on low base rates.

The first major change in labour relations that this type of bargaining represented was the idea that conflict or differences of interest were susceptible to a creative resolution. Negotiations between management and labour could be brought to a 'win–win' conclusion, in games' theory terminology, rather than necessarily requiring that if one party won, the other should inevitably lose. Thus it was possible to bring excessive hours of overtime under control, reduce and stabilize labour costs to management's benefit at the same time as maintaining or increasing workers' earnings, giving them shorter working hours and increased leisure. Indeed because of the way in which a vast number of different changes have been brought about in this manner – changes in which short-term or immediate increases in labour productivity played a very small and often in management's judgement the least important part – it is more useful to regard this practice as creative bargaining for change rather than productivity bargaining. It is this idea that deserves to be the legacy of enduring value that productivity bargaining leaves to the practice of labour relations. But under the broad umbrella of that idea yet other important changes took place that were of lasting value to the management of innovation.

Perhaps the most important of these is the way in which management had to change its ideas about prerogatives in bringing about the changes. Traditionally, management has been concerned to differentiate between those aspects of employment, work and conditions which are proper for negotiation and those where they hold joint consultation to be more appropriate. Perhaps naturally, in so far as they have been concerned to maximize their own autonomy and discretion, they have tried to keep negotiable issues – ones in which they have to reach agreement before change can be made – to an absolute minimum and to relegate all other issues to the joint consultative area, where they are prepared to listen but accept no obligation to pay any attention. Thus they have generally been prepared to accept that as far as earnings, conditions, hours and individual grievances are concerned there may be some intrinsic conflict of interest between employers and employees which can only be resolved by collective bargaining and agreement acceptable to all parties. On the other hand, they have argued or assumed that all other areas are ones of common interest, about which management knows best and that therefore management should exercise its prerogative to manage over these other areas. Thus, management has tended to hold firm to the idea that, for instance, overtime working, manning levels, methods of working, staff grading and so on were all its sole prerogative. But the need to change the level of overtime working in a dramatic way, and the need to change manning levels, methods of working and job grading, quickly brought them to realize that they could often generate change only by agreement and this often meant joint problem solving, job regulation and negotiation over the whole range of issues.

Moreover they found that, if the agreements were to be relevant, meaningful and workable, then they had to be made at the plant level where they were going to operate and with the people who were going to operate them. Thus our studies have shown a striking increase in the degree of plant bargaining in bringing about such agreements. Having accepted that agreements had to be reached at plant level it became necessary to bring into being the institutions through which they could be made.

As we develop in the next chapter, the existing common pattern of formal negotiation was quite inadequate. This often consisted of separate unions representing different groups of workers over 'union' or negotiable matters, in parallel with formal or informal consultation, often with a separate elected body, over 'non-union' matters. But these fragmented and separate channels were quite unsuitable when detailed new job descriptions, systems of organization, payment methods and job-evaluation systems had to be discussed, thrashed out and agreed. They had to be, in the last instance at least, discussed and agreed with people empowered to make agreements involving changes in hours, conditions and earnings, which, in all situations where unions were recognized, meant union officers or, in effect, shop stewards. Moreover these union officers had to be representative of the whole workforce for which they spoke. Again, as the changes cut across all union and work boundaries it would be useful if they agreed the changes with all unions together in a common body.

Thus in order to bring about change, management had to encourage a completely new pattern of collective bargaining and set of institutions. In effect it had to encourage the development of the strong, representative and informed union as the single channel of representation and involvement. Workers were encouraged to join their union in places where there was not a 100 per cent membership. Shop stewards had to be appointed where they did not exist, or did not exist in sufficient numbers, because management needed plenipotentiary representatives with whom to discuss and agree changes. Moreover they had to be given facilities and training to carry out the job. They had to have the opportunity to arrange meetings and have discussions in work time and on work premises in order to give as many of the workers as possible the chance to have a say and make their views known. They had to be given more information about the working of the plant than ever before. Thus a lot of the reforms that many people, including progressive managers and trade unionists, had been demanding for years – shop-steward training, better facilities for carrying out their job, means of making branch decisions more representative, and a greater sharing of information – were brought about because they were necessary to do the job.

Not only did these reforms come about but also the new institutions that we have discussed, the joint working parties and multi-union negotiating committees, were introduced to discuss, negotiate and agree the new agreements. These covered a far wider range of issues than had previously been the subjects of collective bargaining. The distinction between negotiation and consultation had *de facto* become obsolete, and management had recognized that to get the right decisions taken, accepted and implemented was more important than prerogatives; that they could not get change unless all parties accepted change and were prepared to play their part, which required reaching agreement across the whole range of issues.

From all this we can extract three main lessons which we take up one by one in the following chapters. First, management can manage only with the consent of the managed, and that consent will increasingly be won only by greater worker involvement in the making of decisions, requiring that agreement be reached on a much wider range of issues than has previously been the case. Secondly, if effective agreements are to be made, they have to be made at the point at which they are going to work, which requires the decentralization of decision making and bargaining. Thirdly, management needs, as much as their workers, strong, trained, informed, representative, shop stewards with the facilities to do their job. Again in view of our customary theme of 'horses for courses' we hardly need to add that these requirements for bringing about change and worker involvement do not necessarily apply to all sectors of industry, but we believe they do and will increasingly apply to large sectors of British industry where the greatest change is needed.

However the one feature of productivity bargaining that has caused the most widespread concern, particularly among trade unionists at a time of high unemployment, is the reductions in manning and the loss of job opportunities they involved. We have seen how in the petro-chemical case the reduction in the total pool of jobs was the chief source both of resistance to the agreement and of lasting reservations about it. In the ICI Gloucester case manning was reduced by 25 per cent and although this was achieved through natural wastage and voluntary severance such a major loss of jobs is becoming increasingly unacceptable to trade unionists at a time when they see so many out of work. What this point underlines is that if workers and trade unionists are to be expected to become involved in major change programmes that among many other features involve lost job opportunities, it is necessary to ensure a framework of full employment and a buoyant economy. The damage that unemployment and the threat of unemployment impose on creative collective bargaining is enormous.

The men in the middle

In our discussion of total-involvement programmes for change we have tended to focus on management (usually meaning senior management), workers and their representatives. In doing so we have been guilty, by omission, of much the same error as many senior managers. We have forgotten the men in the middle: the supervisor or foreman, junior and middle management. Our enquiries have shown again and again that while senior management, shop stewards and workers have been delighted, even euphoric, about the changes wrought by high-involvement initiatives, their euphoria has been anything but mirrored by the men in the middle. This has been even more marked when a productivity agreement was involved. Indeed there are repeated examples of how supervisors and middle management can become the most dissatisfied groups. They see shop stewards and workers being increasingly courted by senior managers, increasingly involved in planning and designing change, while they themselves are ignored or neglected. They see the importance, status, responsibility and influence of stewards rising while their own declines. When on top of this they see workers being given what they consider massive pay increases, because, as they see it, workers had previously been inefficient, unco-operative and lazy, then pique becomes righteous indignation. While the undeserving idle are fawned upon and rewarded in this way, their virtue goes unrewarded. They, who feel they have always given the company complete loyalty, unquestioning co-operation and unrestrained effort, see their differentials being whittled away and the problems in the jobs increased as they are required to operate an agreement that they played no part in designing and whose basic assumptions and principles they do not accept. Like the prodigal son's brother they cannot help feeling deep resentment at the killing of the fatted calf for the return of the prodigal, while the dutiful, faithful and conscientious son goes without honour. These same feelings and attitudes are often shared by white-collar workers and have no doubt contributed strongly to the rise in the unionization of supervisors and white-collar workers.

A good example of such feelings among supervisors is presented dramatically by the contrasting views of supervisors and shop stewards in yet another case we looked at, which set out to bring about higher steward involvement in the design of change and greater worker involvement in the organization of work after the changes.

The agreement here had been initiated in a situation of bad and worsening labour relations. A new works' general manager and industrial relations' manager were brought in, committed to introducing new plant productivity agreements within twelve months. They saw their major task to improve relations with the shop stewards and involve them heavily in the design of the changes. The agreement was introduced within the time set and implemented successfully. But the difference between the evaluations of the different parties was striking. The stewards took this view:

Relations with top management have changed beyond recognition. We got new people and we've got a new trust. They gave the impression we were on the same level as them. We're calling each other by our christian names. It's very informal. They're always talking to you and they'll always listen to you.

Before there was no trust. You couldn't trust a word they said. You were always asking yourself: where's the snag? where's the trick? You were always looking for the sting in the scorpion's tail. You'd have a meeting with them and you'd go back to a branch meeting and the blokes wouldn't believe a word of it, and you couldn't blame them. Management wouldn't even honour written agreements. Now you can rely on them to stand by verbal agreements.

It was a completely new attitude. Before they tended to make you feel you were something lower than muck. But now they take the attitude, 'We're all one and we've got to get it in, and we've got to get it in together.'

I never believed that attitudes could change like they have here in the last couple of years. That we could co-operate like we have. The idea that we could work together for the same ends and both get something out of it. I never thought I'd see that. I always looked on management as a battle. Never trust them an inch. Don't believe a word they say. And get as much out of them as you can. Cut their throats before they cut yours.

Now you can have a good beef whenever you want to. If anything is bothering you, you can talk it over and get an answer. You may be wrong. It may be something very minor. But you get it off your chest and you get an answer. Beforehand you had to have a branch meeting, cause a great stir, threaten to walk out, make a big thing of it before you could get anything done. Now we have a pow-wow every week. Anything wrong and we get an answer. Beforehand things used just to build up and up until you had a big blow up. Now they're sorted out before they make a big blow up. We have one or two meetings a week. We're getting more and more involved all the time. We're doing more than the supervisors – trying out new ideas, trying out new processes. Trouble is you're working so hard as a steward that you forget about the job. And you make enemies. I don't know what my life would be worth if top management left.

This paean of praise for top management and shop stewards' assessment that relationships and attitudes had been transformed in a positive way contrasts sharply with the views of the supervisors:

I'll tell you straight away this agreement has been a disaster. We've got nothing out of it and now we're stuck with it. There's only one solution — close the place down and start up again somewhere else. That's the only thing to do. They're running this place the shop stewards. They get everything they want. Management gives into them every time. We can't do anything. We can't tell a man off. We can't tell him what to do. We can't sack him. He can't lose any money. We're helpless.

The first thing we knew about it the shop stewards were attending meetings. We were never considered, we were never consulted. All that we got was when it was all finished we were told, 'These rules will apply.' What rules? We weren't even told what the rules were but we were supposed to apply them. It must have been going six months before we got the rules and regulations.

We were conned into this. We didn't get anything that we couldn't have got under national agreement. It's all in the rule book. Why not stick by the rule book? You've got national agreements on shift working, you've got national agreements on transfer of labour. But we've thrown the rule book out of the window and we've got nothing in its place. We've paid through the nose for nothing.

They must be laughing all the way to the bank — the shop stewards — they had to think about it — it wouldn't have taken me five minutes to think about it. We paid a fortune and we've got nothing out of it.

Attitudes haven't changed at all. You get no co-operation. You can't get anybody to do anything. It's always, 'But it says in the new agreement.' The company's got nothing out of it. The only people that have got anything out of it is the shop floor.

We've no bloody say at all. Supervision has gone completely. Nobody backs us. Management never backs us. The shop stewards run the department and the men themselves. We've no say and then we're kicked up the arse if anything goes wrong. But all we do is pass work.

They try these new things out and then we've got to cut down to make up for what they've given away. There comes a point where you've just got to stop. But as I say the only solution here is to close the place down and start again.

And we don't know what's in the new agreement, nobody keeps us in touch, we're supposed to make it work but nobody tells us what's in it. We're so used to the rule book we know it off pat. But we haven't got a clue where we are now. You know you're going to lose whenever anything comes up – they'll have some agreement that you don't know anything about.

The stewards were fully and very perceptively aware of this feeling among supervisors and claimed it was the chief obstacle to the agreement working effectively:

The big stumbling block is middle management. They are the people who've been missed out by top management. Although you're working 40 hours a week with managers and supervisors you never have anything to do with them in negotiations. You do that with top management and then middle management are given some deal signed and settled that they've got to work. And then it may be quite impractical on the shop floor because they don't want to work it.

Management did a good PR job on us. They'd be around every day talking – talking about this and talking about that. It might be talking about nothing in particular. You might think it was a waste of time. But they were talking to you and they were talking to you as an equal. They were treating you as an intelligent human being. And they were listening.

But they didn't do a good PR job on the supervisors. We were consulted and they weren't and that upsets them. So they're taking it out on us. As soon as the bonus came through the complaints started to come in – this was wrong – that was wrong – everything was wrong according to them.

What was intended was we should help to make decisions – our opinion should be taken into account. But they take the attitude, 'Imagine him telling me. What's he doing? He's only working a machine. I'm a supervisor.' But we know our job and we could tell them a thing or two. With this new deal there's something in it for us so we're putting forward new ideas. But they're not interested. You're beating your head against a brick wall. The trouble is it makes him look soft when he's been managing the department for 20 years and a man on the shop floor comes along and tells him how to do the job. If they've not introduced the change themselves top management will think they're not doing the job. Naturally they're resistant to change. They're on a hiding to nothing. When you're talking to top management you're talking to a different class of people. Top management and shop floor work together and middle management are frightened of both.

You can't get the same relationship with middle management as the top. They've got that much to fear and we've got nothing to fear. They're being hounded from both ends. They're frightened someone is doing them out of a job. Where can they go? They can't go up and they won't go down even for more money.

Things have changed and they don't like it. Before you were a cog in a machine. They said jump and you jumped, walk and you walked, run and you ran. That's changed and they don't like it.

Trouble is they were left out of it. They had it slapped in their lap and told to work it. They were never consulted so they were prejudiced against it from the start.

This pattern has emerged time and time again where top management has set off on programmes of radical change based on high involvement of the shop floor and shop stewards in the design and agreement of the changes and greater involvement too in the organization of work during and after implementation, without considering the role of the first-line and middle managers in either the design stage or the new system of organization. This illustrates well the tendency for management to think in terms of problems rather than of systems. The 'problem' here was seen to be lack of trust and lack of co-operation between shop floor/shop stewards and policy-making and negotiating management. This problem was 'solved' but only at the expense of generating further problems because of failure to take the full over-all organizational implications into account. In this case the failure was understandable and even unavoidable because the new top management found themselves in a position where they had been committed in advance to introducing the new agreement within a short time span. But in many other cases where the same pattern has developed it was avoidable.

It is quite clear that in order for there to be orderly and effective management of change, management will increasingly have to look for ways of ensuring high, shop-floor involvement without neglecting first-line and middle management.

It is for this reason that we identified one of the chief strengths of the Gloucester case as the way in which supervisors were more fully integrated into the collaborative process. It was they who led the shop-floor discussion groups. They, too, received extensive new training in order to enable them to help manage the change programme more effectively, and to prepare them and fit them for the new role that they would have to fulfil in the new organization, now based on much less supervision and fewer supervisors. Senior management avoided the temptation to refuse to trust its middle managers and supervisors and to go over their heads in the mistaken conviction, as Lord Stokes has put it, that, 'If only I could speak to all our employees individually, man to man, I'm sure I could persuade them that what I'm saying, and the things we say need to be done, are right.'

The extent to which many top managers tend to believe this is matched only by the intensity with which the reciprocal conviction is held by many workforces: that if only they could get through to the top, if only they could by-pass the layers of supervision and management blocking their access to the real decision makers, then they would get justice. But these matching sets of beliefs among those at the top and the bottom of the enterprise reflect a misleading illusion at the top, and an emotional quasi-religious belief at the bottom, that somewhere there is a benevolent, omnipotent being who can furnish justice. This is not the reality of life in a large organization.

The point of course is that top management cannot talk to every employee personally; it cannot go over the heads of everybody in the middle on every significant issue and decision. It has to work through delegates in middle management and supervision and, through them, talk to representatives of the workforce. If top management wants the right message and the right decisions to get through, the only way to do this is to ensure that its delegates are trained, equipped and able to do the job they have to do, and that workers' delegates are similarly strong and adequate to represent their members. Thus managers, supervisors and shop stewards have all to be strong, confident and responsible and the last possible way to achieve that is for top management to go over their heads on every important issue and decision. The only way to achieve this end is the opposite course of increasing their area and level of responsibility. Thus, for instance, the CIR report on Standard Telephones and Cables East Kilbride, (Cmnd 4598, 1971) which had suffered a history of escalating unofficial stoppages and deteriorating labour relations, identifies as one of the chief sources of the difficulties the way in which top management descended upon the plant to sort out trouble every time there was a major problem. Although top management managed to resolve the particular problem, it only paved the way for further problems in so far as it undermined the confidence and authority of local management and inhibited them from developing the skill, ability and assurance to deal with difficulties as they arose.

The limitations of total involvement for change

So far in this chapter we have considered different examples of major-change programmes based on higher involvement of workers and workers' representatives. Each of these brought manifest benefit to both management and workers in terms of personal satisfaction and interest as well as financial gains. Each was a particularly sophisticated and far-reaching form of productivity agreement. But what is interesting is the way that in evaluating their achievements management often attached less importance to any short-term increase in labour productivity and more importance to what they considered more lasting and constructive change. They had established improved systems, structures, institutions and relations.

They had introduced a more rational, equitable system of payment that promised greater stability and harmony for the future. They had established a new quality of relationship with workers' representatives through involvement in joint problem solving and working out agreements that were mutually advantageous in areas of central importance to both parties. They had established procedures and institutions through which change could be generated, and relationships that were favourable to the bringing about of changes. These we consider further in the next chapter.

Here we need only append the *caveat* that there are limitations to the appropriateness and the practicability of the approaches we have described here. At the 'soft' end of the spectrum that we identified in the last chapter, it may seem incredible to managers that management should have to win the consent of the managed to the types of changes we have described, through negotiation, reaching agreement and sharing the benefits of change. Management at that end of the spectrum finds itself in a situation where unilateral, management decision making is accepted as quite legitimate. It can introduce such changes on the basis of a worker involvement limited to consultation and discussion, combined with the acceptance by workers that their co-operation and acceptance of management's right to make change is adequately and equitably rewarded by annual wage or salary increases that keep them well up with – or well ahead of – earnings in general. It is not surprising that managers in these types of workplaces have often thrown up their hands in horror at the ideas inherent in the types of agreements that we have described here, which they have felt could only increase resistance to change and generate new restrictive practices.

There are equally rigid limitations on the application of this type of approach at the other, 'hard' end of the spectrum. At that end workers and trade unionists, when invited to take the opportunity to become involved in the design of changes, have refused to do so. They have argued that they could play no part in the formulation of changes that would ultimately become the subject of negotiation. They have put the view to management, 'You tell us what you want and we'll tell you whether we will accept it and if so how much it will cost you'. They have feared that if they become too involved, or were seen to become too involved, in the design of changes prior to negotiation, then they might be too predisposed to the changes in advance to get the best deal for their members. At the least they might be seen by their members to be 'management men' and too brainwashed and committed to represent them adequately.

They have defined management's role as involving the responsibility to take decisions, and the union's role as that of opposing, challenging and obstructing decisions if it feels that they are not in its members' interests. This they have argued gives them more influence and power over decisions rather than less, because by becoming involved with management in joint decision making, the design of changes and the formulation of policy, they are in danger of being manipulated, sold the management viewpoint and of having their will, desire and opportunity to oppose decisions sapped. Indeed some commentators on industrial democracy have endorsed this view and argued that workers' interests and involvement in decision making can only properly and effectively be achieved through workers within trade unions acting as a strong, effective opposition to management, on the same model as parliamentary democracy. This argument, we believe, is belied by the cases we have described and we take up the argument again in Chapter Seven.

It is sufficient now to say that where workers do take this view of the opportunity for constructive involvement it is perhaps a natural fear in a situation where the union has in the part been allowed to fulfil no role other than that of opposing, or where it has had reasons for mistrusting management's motives and strategies. To change relationships in this context is a slow and difficult business and will not be achieved overnight merely by offering the opportunity to become involved in one set of changes.

The third type of situation where initiatives for greater worker involvement have failed does not fit easily, anywhere along our spectrum. It includes plants where workers have been too little involved or interested in what goes on at their work to become concerned in change and improvement. For instance one large, television-assembly plant that we looked at, employing mainly women, had set up a scheme whereby local increases in earnings, above the nationally agreed minima, would be based on savings brought about by discussions with work groups. The savings accruing from the first year's operation had not been sufficient even to finance the setting up of the scheme. Here it looked likely that workers' personal investment in their jobs was so slight that they did not respond to the opportunity that the scheme presented.

This confirms Likert's suggestion that it is dangerous to move

suddenly from an authoritarian to a democratic style of management, as it often just results in uncertainty, insecurity, uneasiness
and resistance. (Likert, 1961) We do not, however, accept the
general conclusion that Likert draws from this, that management
should move gradually along its continuum, starting at no participation until it ultimately reaches full participation. We do not
accept this because all the signs are that management is generally no
longer in a position to control the pace of events, to decide how
much participation it is going to permit. Increasingly workers will
demand it and, if it is to continue to manage effectively,
management must respond to and anticipate these demands. It is for
these reasons that, accepting all its limitations, we conclude that the
approach described in this chapter is relevant to a large and growing
sector of British industry.

6 Involvement on a continuous basis: the integration of bargaining and joint consultation

In the last chapter we discussed a number of successful examples of effective employee involvement. These were successful in terms of both the chief criteria we used to identify the need for such involvement: the economic and social objectives. Management was able to make the changes that were necessary for its business to operate more efficiently and smoothly. At the time workers gained markedly increased opportunities to have a say over a crucial sector of their lives.

But, at the risk of incurring the wrath of the managers and trade unionists who sweated blood and tears to make them successful (men who, after they had recounted to us how successful and worthwhile the process had been, sighed, 'But I wouldn't like to have to go through all that again – not for another ten years, anyway'), it has to be said that in some senses these initiatives were relatively easy compared with the over-all problem of establishing continuous employee involvement in decision making. And they were relatively easy because they were concerned with major and dramatic change: dramatic change that had a direct and immediate relevance to many of the most important elements of men's jobs, their level of earnings, their patterns of work, their work-load, their job content, their status and their hours of working. It is in the event of such dramatic changes that employees particularly want a say in decisions that affect them so crucially. Moreover during periods of change there is an atmosphere abroad that can modify the conventional authority system and generate interest and even excitement. This is well captured by the account by a petro-chemical process worker of the kinds of events that he found most rewarding in his work:

The thing I like best is when you're commissioning a new plant. Everybody's on equal par – nobody knows what's going to happen – you're all starting equal. Superintendents, foremen and m:n – you're starting together – you're swopping ideas – your ideas are as good as the next man's. It's far more interesting and we seem to be that much keener. You can put forward your ideas the same as the superintendents and foremen and your ideas are as good as his. They know more technically but they don't know the ins and outs of the plant like you do. It's the same with start-ups and shut-downs – the operator is more conversant with plant than the superintendent. You feel part of it when the superintendent says, 'Now the next thing is so-and-so – how do we go about that?' You feel part of it and you feel you're an equal – everybody's ideas are equal and welcome.

To achieve a high level of involvement in these circumstances requires only that management has the will and the ability to devise the appropriate machinery. It does not have to stimulate the desire for involvement. This is a very different matter from achieving a high level of involvement on a continuing basis when little of great moment is happening or likely to happen.

The need for involvement on a continuous basis.

In view of this it might be asked why it should be so desirable and necessary to provide channels for involvement on a continuous basis. If the most widespread spontaneous demand for involvement is confined to the desire for, firstly, greater control over the day-to-day decisions that affect the day-to-day job, and secondly a greater influence over the shape of major and dramatic change, then it might be thought sufficient to enrich the job to its limits, provide for participative supervision and mount special involvement programmes whenever there are particular changes that affect jobs directly and substantially. The simple answer to this is the quite practical one that it just does not work that way for three reasons.

First, carrying out a programme of total involvement for major change, such as those we have described, changes attitudes, relationships and expectations in a fundamental and irreversible way. It is just not possible for management to revert to its traditional style even if it wanted to – and in all honesty it very rarely wanted to. Indeed, often, one of the chief aims of the programmes was as much to change management styles as radically as the workers' attitudes and practices. But even if this were not the case, even if management had been acting out of consideration of purely short-term, practical goals, it finds that it has to change also. The process of involvement in the change, and relationships with management during that process, generate expectations among workers and their representatives which require it. The experience of involvement leads them to want and expect continued and even greater involvement. They come to expect to be consulted about change, rather than having decisions taken unilaterally and imposed upon them. They expect to be asked rather than instructed to carry out tasks. The fact that so many doors have been opened to them in the change programme leads them to question those doors that still remain shut, whereas previously they may have taken it for granted that all doors were shut.

This is well illustrated by the views of middle management and shop stewards respectively in their evaluation of one ICI WSA application that we looked at. One plant manager put it this way:

There's a completely new attitude among the men. Before they suffered in silence. Now they'll shout, 'What the hell's going on?' That's a good thing. We've taught them to expect to be told and now they want to be told. That means that the 'gen sessions' (monthly meetings to discuss past and future operations) are worthwhile. They're interested in them and they want to contribute to them.

This theme was taken up by a foreman in accounting for why management had failed to get a proposal for the individual counselling of workers over their sickness and absenteeism records accepted:

But we just sprung it on them and you just can't spring anything on them any more. Every time that we've tried to spring something on them we've come unstuck. You just can't choose the things you want to do and are going to do because you're management, and the things you're going to consult about. Once you've started on consultation you've got to go the whole way. You've got to consult on everything or if you don't you'll come unstuck.

It has to be added that not all his colleagues had yet learned this lesson, but that enough of them had, to bring about a fundamental change in style of management on a continuing basis, is suggested by this view by the senior process shop steward:

It's much easier to discuss things now. Beforehand you couldn't talk to anybody. It was stand to attention, 'Yes Sir, No Sir', sort of thing. Now you can get a hearing whenever you want and they do consult you before there's any change. As far as we're concerned everything is discussed and agreed. We have regular meetings. We're told what the work load is going to be and we agree the way it's going to be tackled. All the work-study figures are given to process shop stewards and agreed before any job is done. And everything is discussed with us before there's any change. Any change on the process is discussed with the men first. New valves or vessels – it's discussed with the men. There'd be hell to pay now if they didn't. It's common sense really if somebody asks you to do something, or asks for your suggestions how to do it, you go along with them. If they come along saying, 'Do this, Do that, Do the other', well you tell them, 'Get stuffed'.

It is true that his colleagues in the craft unions felt less strongly that the pattern of involvement in decision making established in the change programme had been continued into the operating phase. In particular they felt that the system of centralized maintenance planning that had been set up restricted both their opportunities and those of their members for involvement, and, associated with this, ensured that they worked very much less effectively than they might. Moreover all stewards felt that there still remained much more scope for their constructive involvement. For example: 'Things have opened up a lot but they could be opened up a lot further. We have our plant gen sessions but they still hold a lot of their cards close to their chest. I think we'd have a lot to contribute if we went to the foremen's gen sessions.'

These comments highlight the way in which involvement creates the appetite for more involvement and how management, once it has created certain expectations about its behaviour, has to be consistent in order to fulfil those expectations. The comments also indicate something of how this can work out in practice.

This leads us on to the second main reason why management

cannot merely use involvement, in the event of major change, and forget about it once the change is successfully implemented. If such programmes are set up solely in the event of particular significant changes, which in practice means when management has something it wants to change, without any provisions being made for joint job regulation and joint decision making on a permanent and continuing basis, then there is a tendency for these processes to come to be seen as manipulative. Management is seen as using involvement purely as a technique, to gain compliance with its decision whenever it has a particularly difficult problem, but as unprepared to share power and control on a more permanent basis.

The machinery for involvement is invoked only when management needs or wants to involve its workforce. Workers' ideas and views are exploited when it suits management's book but are ignored otherwise.

Thus there have been cases of very successful total-involvement exercises for change which have been followed by resistance to change and non-participation at a later date because the machinery set up for the first exercise has been allowed to lapse. Similarly we have seen how some trade unionists and workers have been reluctant to participate in particular change exercises because such participation is inconsistent with their regular and continuing relationship with management.

Thus it is clear that once management has set out upon the course defined by this type of total-involvement programme, this leads directly to the need to establish provisions for involvement, for joint decision making and for joint regulation on a permanent and continuous basis. It is true, as we have mentioned, and as we shall see again, that one of the chief problems with keeping alive the machinery and the attitudes necessary for this to be successfully achieved is how to stop everybody from dying of boredom when nothing of great moment or drama is happening in the business, or nothing of substance is being changed in the workplace. But just as the need for change provides the chief practical rationale for greater worker involvement in decision making from management's point of view, so the need for change will create the chief practical opportunity for involvement. And it is clear that the foreseeable future is going to demand an accelerated rate of change. The speed of technological and technique innovation, coupled with British management's past failures even to keep its practices up to date, should be sufficient to ensure that there is ample opportunity for worker involvement in decision making and that any machinery set up has quite enough to do to maintain effective involvement.

Thirdly, beyond these practical considerations for maintaining involvement on a continuous basis and as well as the requirement that if management wants the opportunity of a high level of involvement in particular instances it has to maintain it permanently, there are, of course, further reasons for providing such channels other than increased participation in the workplace and in the event of major change. The chief of these is that many decisions that affect employees are taken at a level far removed from the workplace, and if they are going to have a say in decisions that affect them, their views and interests need to be represented at those levels.

New institutions for involvement

Some of the ways of bringing about both continuous involvement and the required new institutions have already been touched on in our illustrative quotations at the beginning of this chapter. They can be further developed by reference to the Gloucester case, for here management was satisfied that, apart from the striking increases in productivity, and the degree of job enrichment and enhanced job satisfaction achieved, perhaps the major long-term benefit experienced as a result of the exercise was the improvement of labour relations and the forging of new machinery for consultation and negotiation that were enabling that improvement to be maintained. Before the agreement the arrangements had been typical of those in many progressive British firms. There had been a traditional, elected works' council as the chief consultative body with very limited terms of reference – nothing which might become a negotiating matter could be discussed. Parallel to, but separate from, this there was the usual formal system of trade-union representation and negotiation through general and craft unions. As we have seen, these distinct media for consultation and negotiation had proved quite inadequate, as in so many other cases, for introducing the changes, and the shop-floor discussion groups, shift meetings and joint working party had been set up under a new joint negotiating body made up of lay officers from all unions. These innovations have now been formalized and established on a permanent basis as a system of interlocking consultative groups on the Likert model. They consist of the shop-floor discussion groups (the gen sessions referred to above), shift meetings and a works' council now composed of shop stewards, as a single channel of involvement and representation. Any meeting can discuss any subject and it is only when a consensus is not reached, or either party requests it, that the matter becomes one for formal negotiation. Management feels that it has thus established effective channels for two-way communication, and for sorting out problems, issues and grievances before embitterment occurs and without the parties being required to take up formal defensive negotiating stances. The chief measure of the effectiveness of these changes that managers were able to cite eighteen months after the agreement was that, while three new processes had been introduced since then, the personnel manager had not been involved in one negotiation during that period, whereas previously he had continually been involved in them. The new institutions, backed by the experience line management had had of operating them while introducing the agreement, together with the training in industrial relations this had given them, enabled them to anticipate, prevent or deal with issues as they arose. The fact that three new processes had been introduced over this period meant that the absence of disputes and changed role of the personnel department did not reflect a period of stability and consolidation following the agreement. It was, however, helped by the way in which the new system of payments, a weekly salary, replacing an unpopular PBR scheme, had reduced the potential sources of dispute.

The new institutions that developed out of this change programme have become the general pattern for ICI, with their work-group discussions and plant discussions or 'gen sessions' and their restructured works' councils, which include shop stewards and have substantially increased powers.

As we shall see these developments have been widely paralleled elsewhere within firms and plants where management set out to bring about major change; found, as we have demonstrated, that many of the distinctions between negotiating and consultative areas and bodies were inadequate for change; and subsequently found that they were really equally inadequate for normal operations.

The substantial movement, then, towards the concept of the single channel of representation, ultimately the trade union, hinges upon recognition of the impracticability of distinguishing between what are exclusively consultative, as opposed to negotiating, issues and of management standing firm on any unilateral decision making prerogatives. The movement also represents a recognition that joint consultation as a self-contained concept and purely joint consultative works' councils have generally failed and failed lamentably. The last chapter exposed all their inadequacies as a medium for change but this only highlights the ineffectiveness of such bodies all over western Europe. Joint consultative bodies have tended to degenerate rapidly and quickly to come to be seen as talking shops concerned with trivial matters such as cold chips in the canteen, without powers to deal with important issues. They have thus rapidly created disillusionment among managers, workers and their representatives with ideas of increased worker involvement through such means. Reviewing these failures Blumberg (1968) concludes that it is clear that 'the direct involvement of workers must take place within institutions that have significant powers.'

Thus if works' councils are to become effective institutions for worker involvement they must concern themselves and have power to deal with issues and topics that are important to workers. But bringing this about quickly introduces, directly or indirectly, consideration of grievances, procedures, earnings and conditions. And if the works' council is going to consider topics such as these, then it has to be composed of workers' representatives who already make agreements on behalf of workers on these topics: lay officers of the trade unions or shop stewards – at least in situations where unions are recognized. This brings us straight back to the single channel of representation and the integration of joint consultative and negotiating institutions. All the reasons for taking this course were summed up for us quite simply by the personnel manager who explained why his company had decided to integrate the previously separate channels: 'If you have one body that is purely a negotiating body, every time you sit down with them at a table they say 'No', and they expect cash for saying 'Yes'. And if you have another body that is purely a consultative body they get bored and go to sleep.'

What this also highlights is how the existence of separate channels ensures that the workers' representative body that has some power, and can exercise power, can exercise it only in a negative, obstructive way. As we argue in the next chapter, if management casts the union purely in the role of opposition, and gives it no scope other than to defend and promote the interests of its members in situations explicitly recognized by management as in conflict with those of the employer, management can hardly be surprised if all that the union does is oppose, obstruct and resist management initiatives. Similarly, separate channels also ensure that the body which represents the area that management chooses as one of congruence of interests is weak and ineffectual, and dies of irrelevance and boredom. Any constructive contribution that worker involvement could bring about is dissipated.

For instance the CIR report on STC East Kilbride identified as perhaps the single biggest source of the troubles the way in which management tried to maintain a firm distinction between joint consultation and negotiation (a distinction which the Commission clearly recognized as largely meaningless in principle and self-defeating in practice), and refused to negotiate on a wide range of issues. And the chief recommendation for change in institutions and procedures was for the separate channels to be replaced by a Joint Works' Committee as a single channel of representation through which comprehensive plant agreements should be negotiated. (Report No. 14 Cmnd. 4598, 1971)

The alternative management starting point to the one adopted by STC Kilbride is that expressed to us by the chairman of the Rod Division of the Delta Metal Company whose integrated system of representation we studied:

We are not concerned with management prerogatives. Our primary concern is to get the right decisions taken and accepted. You can't achieve change unless all parties accept change and are prepared to play their part in it. This involves bargaining and consultation over the whole range of issues. The distinction between bargaining and consultation is largely meaningless in practice. The only management prerogative is to initiate discussion.

This is the view that we suggested was implicit in those major change programmes that we have discussed though rarely has it been expressed so explicitly and consciously as this. Indeed the idea that the 'only management prerogative is to initiate discussion' may seem so radical and dangerous to management that it is worth spelling out what it does and does not mean in practice in the Rod Division of Delta. It does *not* mean that every time management wants to do or change anything it then sits down in eyeball-to-eyeball confrontation with the unions and engages in a process of horse trading, compromise and bargaining over money. Indeed the credo is specifically based on the desire to avoid this. It recognizes the real change in the nature of industrial power over the last ten years and the quickening shop-floor awareness of the power it has. It recognizes also the rising demand for involvement in decision making, and above all that unless management takes the initiative in satisfying that demand then it will find itself in a stranglehold. Unless it devises means of getting worker involvement in reaching the right decisions, initiates ways of getting agreement about change and ways of introducing change so that it can carry its workpeople with it, then the unions will take the initiative in demanding that there be no change without agreement. Management will then be left foolishly standing firm on its 'rights', which have little basis in principle and none in practice, will have to face demands for the maintenance of the *status quo* until new agreements are reached, and will them have to sit down in direct confrontation every time it wants to change.

What this chairman is saying is that nothing will be achieved by proclaiming or defending rights or prerogatives. Progress will stem from the practical attitude of working out how decisions can best be reached which affect all aspects of people's work and that accommodate the differing interests in the organization, and how the company can best get these decisions agreed, accepted and implemented. It accepts that this will involve bargaining across the board. But it has a very different idea of bargaining from the popular one, which conceives of this only in terms of cash and compromise. For Rod Division it involves taking soundings to identify differences of value and interest, the development of proposals that seek to resolve those differences, the discussion of proposals to isolate and accommodate outstanding differences and the reaching of agreement upon the best solution. The mechanics of this process are as follows.* At divisional level management meets regularly with full-time union officers to discuss very informally its future planning and thinking. This is to ensure that when plans and policies are first being formulated there is an output of ideas from people with a

---

* Our account of Delta Metal institutions, practices and experiences are based upon and confined to the Rod Division, one of six largely autonomous Divisions in the group. The other Divisions are, however, moving in much the same direction.

trade-union, industrial-worker viewpoint. Indeed it can be suggested that full-time union officers are here fulfilling very much the role that we cast for them in talking of non-executive workers' directors. But this is a complete reversal of the more common management attitude of wanting nothing to do with full-time officers, of preferring to deal with their own shop stewards alone, of regarding it as a failure if the full-time officer has to be called in, and therefore proudly proclaiming that they have not seen a full-time officer for years. Whatever else this may achieve, it also ensures that when they do see one they have anything but a good working relationship to build on.

The next stage is a central (Divisional) works' council, having the chairman of the Division as its chairman in order to demonstrate the importance that is attached to the council, and composed of senior shop stewards from the different works as well as top, Divisional-management representatives. There is no attempt to balance the numbers of shop steward and management representatives. This it is felt would only contribute to a sense of confrontation. Thus, as in all the Division's other works' councils, shop stewards are in a large majority on the central works council. The function of this body is to feed in information on the plans and performance of the Division, to take up any problems that have not been resolved at plant works' council level, and to negotiate agreements on matters that are common to the Division. In so far as the Division pursues a conscious policy of decentralization of decision making to plant level there is not a great deal to be negotiated at this level. But there has been a determined effort in the recent past to develop procedural agreements that are consistently applied throughout the Division. And the central works' council has played a useful part in this. For instance it has served a particularly useful role in the problems and redundancies brought about by the closure of a plant in the Division. For management this was brought home strongly when the senior shop steward at the plant, interviewed on television, said that he and his members had been strongly tempted to resist the closure by direct action and that they would have done so had they not had the central works' council through which to make their protest known and through which to ensure the minimum hardship for workers. We consider some aspects of this again when we look at other joint institutions.

Again the central works' council had been instrumental in

bringing about an 'expatriate agreement'. The suggestion had been put up from among the Division's large number of Commonwealth immigrant workers that they should have provision for extended leave in order to visit families in their country of origin, while being assured that their jobs would still be open when they returned. Management was sympathetic to the idea in principle while feeling that it would create a substantial problem in practice. Similarly, other groups of workers in the organization had mixed feelings about it, and some felt that such a change would represent preferential treatment for the black minority or 'racial discrimination in reverse'. Thus this was a conflict situation in the sense we have used the term. The suggestion highlighted differences of interest between one group of workers and other groups on the one hand, and management and workers on the other. Yet an 'expatriates leave' agreement was successfully negotiated through the central works' council that sought to minimize inconvenience to management, give all workers with families of origin in overseas countries the right to extended leave for visits, and satisfy all groups of workers that no one was being preferentially treated. This little example illustrates resolution of conflict through negotiation, made possible by appropriate institutions, just as much as does the ending of a six-week strike through a compromise solution, although unfortunately people all too often tend to think immediately of the second type of situation rather than of the first, when hearing the terms 'conflict' and 'negotiation'.

The third level in the Division's institutions is the level that it would consider the most important. This is the plant works' council. As mentioned, the Division has a firm policy of decentralization to plant level and sees the plant works' council as the main body for the joint regulation of decisions across the board at plant level. Once again it is chaired by the works' chief executive, and is made up of nominated shop stewards who are in a majority. It includes staff and supervisory shop stewards and there has been a conscious group policy of encouraging staff and supervisors to become unionized. Again the new structure has superseded the separate channels of elected, consultative works' council and negotiating shop stewards, on the basis of the reasoning put forward above. The committee is seen as the body which negotiates all terms, conditions and procedures that are decided at plant level. It is fully recognized that if it is going to work it has to have powers, has to consider important issues and has to have strong meat to feed on. As the deputy chairman of the division puts it:

We hope to move steadily in the direction of giving works' committees more of a role in procedures. They are, of course, representative of all the unions and through them it is possible to discuss problems from the point of view of the needs of the whole factory community. In the long run this is important to us. We wish to promote the standing and importance of our works' committees. We see them as the focal point of our relationships with the representatives of employees and through them with the employees themselves. In many of our factories they are already functioning in this key, central capacity.

For instance, the works' committee acts as the final court of appeal in the plant, before going to arbitration, within the disciplinary agreement. Thus disputes over misconduct and discipline are the subjects of appeal to a body on which the majority are union representatives.

In the same way there is the provision for sub-committees to deal with subjects of special interest, or those relating to particular groups of workers which are of little interest to the full committee. One example of this was the hardship committee set up following the closure of the plant that we referred to. This was a body to which any redundant employee could appeal who felt his redundancy had brought about particular hardship or that he had personal problems not catered for in the agreement. The constitution of the works' hardship committee makes provision for a chairman drawn from the Divisional board, the factory general manager and personnel manager together with four employee representatives, two nominated shop stewards and two elected. Again workers' representatives are in the majority. And any unanimous recommendation of the committee to relieve hardshop brought about by transfer or redundancy is binding on the Division.

These then are the types of joint regulatory institutions being set up to pursue the chairman's credo. The chief purpose to which the machinery has been put over the last few years has been to introduce jointly agreed procedural agreements. The starting point had been one of 'indifferent or bad labour relations', characterized by almost monthly visits to York (the last stage of the National Engineering

Procedures), unofficial action and unsatisfactory relationships with shop stewards. The goal had been to establish with shop stewards agreed standards of behaviour, ways of going about things and means of resolving differences, and through this to build up a constructive working relationship with them. Thus, along the lines recommended by Donovan, agreements were worked out on redundancy, grievance and disciplinary procedures, shop stewards' roles and facilities, the application of job evaluation and so on. (Cmnd. 3623, 1968) This had been backed by a joint training programme during which both first-line management and stewards had been separately on the identical courses jointly organized and financed by management and the unions. The chief benefits management saw coming from this process included a virtual end to visits to York, a dramatic reduction in unofficial stoppages, the ability to deal with disciplinary problems effectively and the closure of a plant in an orderly and equitable way that would previously have been quite impossible. At the same time they had established constructive working relationships with union officers both lay and full time at all levels. This was certainly reflected in the attitudes of shop stewards in one plant that we visited. This plant had inherited a far from enviable labour relations situation. As management put it:

This works used to be a family firm where you did what you were told or you got out. We inherited the bitterness that came from that. They realized that they'd got the power now and they were going to get their own back. There was a big growth in unionization because of this rank bad management in the past. But we welcome that growth now and we've encouraged it. It helps management that they've got someone to speak for them – a direct negotiating channel. Agreements stick if everybody's a party to them.

The change was clearly recognized by stewards:

Relations in the Division are second to none and the higher up you go the better you do. Top management believes in trade unions and trade unionism a hundred per cent. They're behind it all the way. It's in the middle that they fall away a bit – so we've got to keep bashing away to make sure they know we're a force to be reckoned with.
But we've got every facility we want. We can call a meeting

whenever we want. We can have the use of an office or a telephone whenever we want. We can phone another shop steward in any other part of the company whenever we want. They've organized courses for us and so on.

It was clear this change did not mean that management yielded to every demand. Indeed stewards made a special point of emphasizing that the change in management that they valued as much as any other was that suddenly it was stronger, more confident, knew where it wanted to go and was taking the initiative. They had not enjoyed a situation where management had been so weak and ineffectual that it caved in to every demand, and chaos ensued. They welcomed a strong management with whom they could get together and make meaningful agreements, but equally a management which saw their role not only as legitimate but also as essential to the smooth running of the business.

The nature of the innovation that had both made these changes desirable and helped to bring them about was rather different from those that we discussed in the last chapter. Here it was confined to procedural agreements, whereas the productivity agreements discussed often included both new procedural and substantive agreements. But they were based on much the same set of assumptions, here made even more explicit, the chief of which was that if orderly, constructive labour relations were to be achieved there had to be an extension of joint regulation. Rather than confining bargaining to wages it had to be extended to all aspects of work behaviour. As the deputy chairman puts it:

We need to change the defensive attitudes that have so often dominated us in the past, replacing them where we can with a constructive relationship. ...our industrial relations should not be dominated by a narrow exchange of views on money, which promotes defensiveness on both sides, but expanded into a wider discussion in which money will be only one of the matters which is under debate. ...We need to start bargaining about conduct and conduct is not money.

Of course this company is not alone in the changes it has brought about in the extension of joint regulation, in the application of this particularly to behaviour through procedural agreements or in the development of an integrated system of representation. The Industrial Society looked at changes that had taken place in formal systems of involvement in a number of firms. (Henderson, 1970) It looked at Tube Investments, Stainless Tubes Limited, Mullards, English China Clay, Cadburys, Hoover and British Steel Corporation–Stockbridge. The cases had a number of common characteristics. First, they had often had traditional elected works' councils which had either ceased to function completely or were in severe decay. Secondly, they had often recently experienced major change programmes which had fully exposed the limitations of the traditional structure for the reasons we have emphasized. Thirdly, they had moved substantially towards a single integrated channel of representation through a reconstituted works' council composed of shop stewards, and had enriched the diet of this council. And, fourthly, where union membership was low they had strongly encouraged employees to join, in order that shop stewards on the council were fully representative.

Similarly the benefits management claimed to have experienced were largely common to them all. The work of the council became meaningful because real issues were discussed. Relationships with stewards were improved enormously through the extension of the range of topics discussed and agreed with them, which now included many where there was a great deal of common ground as well as those where there were strong differences. Co-operation between unions, representing different sections of the workforce, improved through membership of a common body. Moreover there were often direct commercial benefits of the new structure. They had been the instruments for bringing about successful productivity deals or in BSC, as in case quoted above, they had enabled management to reduce its labour force humanely.

We have stressed the benefits for management in such changes, but needless to say in view of our continuing theme that management/labour relations need by no means necessitate a 'win–lose' outcome, there are also clear benefits for workers and trade unions: for workers, the opportunity to have their views and interests promoted and represented over a much wider area and in a much more powerful way than previously; for trade unions the recognition of the union as the chief channel of representation, increasing its scope and influence. Thus in a very successful productivity agreement that we looked at in a Midlands engineering complex, union officers cited the introduction of an integrated system of representation as the chief of the many benefits that they and their members had got out of it. The district officer argued that although the firm had been fully unionized previously, neither men nor management ever took advantage of this because the stewards' position was constantly undermined by the elected works' council.

The chief unresolved problem that emerges from this is our old friend, the role of the men in the middle, which we illustrated in a dramatic way at the end of the last chapter in terms of total change programmes, but which reared its ugly head again in all these examples of institutions for involvement on a continuous basis cited here. Again middle and junior management tended to feel left out and neglected while their job was being eroded. We can only repeat the argument put forward at that point, that management has to think in terms of the whole organization when planning these changes, that it has consciously to work out a role for middle and first-line management in this organization, that this should seek to enrich the job where it has been eroded (it should not be too difficult to compensate for the impoverishment brought about by having intractable, disiciplinary problems reduced for first-line management), and having identified the roles it should be training the managers to fit them.

In concluding this chapter we have to emphasize that we have not been trying to lay down a blueprint of practice and institution that should be taken over completely by every organization. We have been concerned to demonstrate the need for involvement in decision making on a continuous basis. We have described what a number of firms have done to try to establish this. We have seen how the impetus brought about by major involvement for change pro- grammes has been maintained both informally, through greater consultation and discussion between first-line and middle managers, workers and shop stewards, about the way jobs are to be tackled, work allocated and plant manned in day-to-day working on the shop floor, and formally through discussion groups, 'gen sessions' or briefing groups at different levels of the hierarchy. All this has been conducted within the framework of an integrated works' council which may include specialist sub-committees, such as joint disci- plinary, safety, training, manpower planning or hardship committees.

We have suggested that there are certain principles inherent in these changes that have a great deal of relevance for managements in large sectors of British industry. These are essentially that management should accept pragmatically what needs to be done in order to get decisions taken, accepted and implemented rather than standing on rights and prerogatives, that this demands the extension of joint regulation across a much wider area than has hitherto been the custom, and that this in turn requires one channel of representation and in effect, where unions are recognized, the trade union as that channel. The emergence of the union as the chief channel of representation makes new and quite different demands upon union members and officers and these we go on to consider in the next chapter.

7 Trade unions as a channel of employee involvement

The need for change and for employees to have a greater say in changes have led increasingly to the establishment for the trade union as the chief or sole channel of representing employees' views, ideas and interests to management. We have described how, given that a high degree of worker involvement in decision making is necessary to management at certain points in time and in certain contexts, then this requires a basis of continuous involvement. Moreover it is desirable that this involvement be manifested through a single channel to avoid a situation where management is faced with, on the one hand, a powerful body that can only obstruct and oppose and, on the other, a weak and ineffectual body incapable of fulfilling any creative, constructive purpose.

Thus the employers concerned, once they had accepted that a higher level of participation in decision making by employees is desirable, have generally, where there has been some recognition of unions, moved inevitably to a situation where the trade union is the natural, the most effective and the most desirable medium for workers' representation if their voices are to be heard. In addition to all the practical considerations quoted that made this desirable for management, there is a further point more often cited by trade unionists. Generally, only within the framework of the union and with the moral backing of a third party separate from the power structure of the enterprise, can the employee talk to management on anything approaching equal terms. If the only frame of reference is the workplace and its organization, then its hierarchy defines him as a subordinate, as someone inferior in responsibility, authority, status and value to the enterprise, and it is difficult to conceive of any practicable business organization where this is not the case. But this locates the employee in a position of dependence, dependent upon the good-will, discretion and patronage of his superiors in a whole range of areas affecting his job and career. Such a context, leaving aside complaints, grievances and conflicts of interest, is not conducive to an atmosphere in which ideas and criticisms that implicitly challenge superiors can be freely expressed. Thus there is a danger in many organizations that managers, who believe they get a true picture of what employees think at all levels of the hierarchy, will find themselves in a similar position to that of the commanding officer who believes that all his troops are quite happy with their food when, on inspecting the canteen, he gets no response to his question 'Any complaints, lads?' with the sergeant-major glowering threateningly at his side.

Thus within a hierarchical organization it seems more likely that the voice of those at the bottom of the hierarchy will be more freely expressed and more effectively heard when backed both by a framework independent of the power, status and reward system of the organization, and ultimately by their collective strength to compensate for the power they cannot have within the formal hierarchy. It is for this reason that trade unionists argue that union membership is essential to the dignity of the worker, because it is the union that stands for the essential human value and rights of the member, independent of the role and status that is ascribed him within the particular organization. With the best will in the world even the best-intentioned management cannot ensure that all members have an equal position when, within a by definition hierarchical context, it attaches different levels of status, power and rewards to different levels.

We outlined in our introduction to this section the way in which some enterprises manage to achieve a relatively open organization, and create an organizational climate where those at all levels have both the opportunity and the encouragement to express their ideas, views and criticisms without union support. But we also pointed out that these companies were unusual in the dedication of top management and training of middle management to this goal; unusual also in their circumstances and structural characteristics and unusual in the composition of their workforce. This located them at one end of the spectrum we defined. For historical and institutional reasons the bulk of enterprises in the middle of the spectrum could not replicate these systems even if they thought it desirable. But many employers and managers among this mainstream group have been reluctant to cast unions in the role that we have gradually been developing for them. They have been reluctant to do so for two main reasons. They resent the intrusion of what they consider to be a third party, the union, intervening between them and their employees, introducing and exacerbating conflict within the enterprise, and infringing management's right to manage. They thus see an extension of negotiation rights and joint regulation as an extension of conflict, a further obstacle to change and a reduction in managerial control. In fact, as we have already described and as we shall see further towards the end of this chapter, accepting this role for unions can facilitate and accelerate change and can give management more effective control because it is shared.

Meanwhile it is worth considering a little further these two managerial reservations concerning an extension of the sphere of joint regulation. First the appeal to 'management's right to manage' can hardly be considered as very much more than a slogan. If what is claimed by this is that managers are the trustees of shareholders, whose ownership of the business gives them the right to decide quite unilaterally, through their managers, everything that happens in that business, then the claim is as invalid in principle as it is counterproductive in practice. Property rights furnish the owner with rights over property not over people. Any right that managers have to manage must in a free society depend on the consent of the managed. That consent may be freely given in return for financial payments alone; in recognition of management's competence, professional and technical expertise; in deference to management's ability to deliver sustained success and to ensure that all groups of employees receive an equitable share of that success; or in response to clear evidence that the ideas, views and interests of employees are taken into account. But equally that consent can be removed if the financial payments are seen not to be equitable, if management is seen to be incompetent, lacking in professional and technical expertise, or pursuing policies that employees consider − whether reasonably or not − to be opposed to their interests. The removal of consent may take the form of quitting or of collectively challenging management's right to unilateral decision making. It is becoming clear that as a result of the social changes which we have identified throughout our report − a better educated, more questioning and demanding workforce; powerful national and international movements among those in subordinate positions in all sectors of society for more influence and power; a breakdown of respect for authority based solely upon position; and the increasingly strong bargaining position of organized labour in relation to capital intensive and large, highly interdependent, industrial complexes — as a result of all these trends management will increasingly have to earn and win the consent of employees to be managed rather than claiming it as of right. As the Director-General of the CBI has expressed it:

Managers do not — if they ever had — have a divine right to manage. There is no automatic prerogative to make decisions and expect them to be carried out. The process of decision making will have to be more and more justified and demonstrated to be right in order to command the respect not only of the people working in the company but the community as a whole. (W.C. Adamson, 1970)

In practice this means that managers in that sector which we have identified as being our main interest who want to retain or recover control will have to learn to share it. At the same time we hardly need add that there are instances where this does not have the same urgency if the rewards and satisfactions furnished by the organiza-tion are quite consistent with what employees seek from their work.

It is, of course, natural that management, like any other group or individual, should want to retain the greatest freedom of action. Management's need to win the consent of a particular group before it can implement a certain policy may prove nearly as frustrating and irritating to the manager as the complete lack of freedom to influence his pace, content or method of work may prove to the operator. But the freedom of management, again like that of any other group or individual, to swing its fist stops very emphatically where somebody else's nose begins. It is clear that there are often conflicts between the interests of employers and employees. Managers have the interests of consumers, suppliers, the local and general community and shareholders, to take into account as well as the interests of different groups of employers. It is hardly conceivable that all the interests of all these groups will coincide all the time.

At the most obvious level the change required to increase productivity and profitability, new methods, new plant, reorganization and rationalization, may make many hard-won, valued and prestigious skills quite obsolete, apart from creating redundancy of both jobs and skills. And apart from any real losses in skill, status, job satisfaction and security brought about by change, the idea may be threatening in itself. For those who are concerned with designing, planning, directing and implementing change, it may well be exciting, challenging, demanding and rewarding. But for those who are planned, directed and managed, change itself may represent a certain disutility in its own right, whether or not they experience any real losses in their jobs after the change has been implemented and is operating. They are the objects, rather than the initiators of change, and for them it means insecurity and uncertainty, something imposed on them, over which they have no control.

Thus conflicts of interest are inherent to hierarchical business organizations which have multiple interests to serve and have to adapt and change. It follows from this that union representation of employees' interests does not introduce conflict into organizations. Rather it reflects the conflict that already exists, institutionalizes it, and provides a medium through which the interests of those at the bottom of the hierarchy can be represented and the conflicts of interest between them and the other parties can be resolved through negotiation which, as we have tried to demonstrate, involves not only compromise and horsetrading, but also the seeking of alternative solutions that serve the interest of all parties.

Indeed once employers recognize that they have responsibilties towards employees and their interests, it is difficult to maintain that it is they rather than directly accountable representatives who should be the sole arbiters of what is good for employees and what employees' interests are. Similarly it would be somewhat inconsistent to accept that employees should have a say in critical decisions that affect them directly, but that management should always decide whether what they say is practicable, useful or desirable and their voice should never be backed by the power or strength which union representation gives.

Thus the extension of joint regulation of the type we have described in the kinds of situation with which we are primarily concerned may appear to impose additional constraints on managerial discretion, and may in fact do so; but also, as we shall further illustrate it can equally enable management to make the types of change that would otherwise be difficult if not impossible. The

extension of union influence in these circumstances reflects rather
than increases conflict and may well enhance rather than mar
employee morale for workers gain a more effective channel through
which their ideas and interests can be represented and seen to be
represented. (Bain, 1967)

Of course, while it is important to recognize that in many
situations the interests and ideas of employers and employees are
often in conflict, and this conflict should properly and usefully be
institutionalized, there is usually also a large area of common
interests. This is widely recognized by trade unionists, who generally
see quite clearly a large area of common interests and are quite able
to differentiate between areas of conflicting and common interests.
For instance, in our study of productivity agreements, we found that
full-time union officers tended to spend more time in supporting and
agreeing with management in the face of opposition to rank and file
shop-floor workers and shop stewards, than they did in opposition
to management. Thus the 'outsiders', the 'third party' whose
intrusion we suggested management resented and sought to avoid,
were more often in accord with management than was management
in accord with its own employees. Again, in the case studies
reported, we described how the operators could quite happily
sustain contradictory images of their relationship with management,
the one being characterized by feelings of 'teamwork', the other by
feelings of conflict, with the images becoming salient depending on
context.

But all too often both managers and social commentators find it
difficult to sustain the simple idea that employees and trade
unionists can recognize and serve both common and conflicting
interests in parallel or even simultaneously. They demand complete
loyalty and when total loyalty is not forthcoming assume absolute
disloyalty and opposition.

Thus management tends to see shop stewards only in an
opposition role when there is trouble. When there is overt and
mutually recognized conflict, the function stewards are allocated is
to oppose and drive as hard a bargain as possible for their members.
Management then tends to assume that their stance in this context
represents their general outlook and that stewards are interested
only in opposing, obstructing and challenging, and in conflict with
management on every issue and topic. (We noted how managers tend
to get a similarly distorted view of what interests people in their jobs

through talking to them in only one set of contexts.) However, as emerged time and time again in the cases to which we referred in the last chapter where management had extended the area of joint regulation, had increased the range of issues and topics discussed with stewards to include the less contentious ones – as in the integrated works' councils – they found that relationships with stewards improved perceptibly and became more constructive. Thus the extension of joint regulation, rather than introducing conflict into areas where previously there had been harmony, brought about a markedly more balanced and reciprocal relationship between management and stewards.

This is exactly what might be predicted from the information that is available on the attitudes of shop stewards, which indicates that they see both a large area of common interests, and a large part of their role as helping management to serve common interests. For instance, in the survey of shop stewards carried out by the Social Survey for Donovan, when respondents were asked to what extent they thought that they as shop stewards helped management to solve its problems and run the firm more efficiently, 68 per cent said 'quite a lot' and only 6 per cent thought they were not helping management at all. Particularly interesting was the way the survey demonstrated that the wider the range and the greater the number of issues upon which they negotiated, the more likely stewards were to think they helped management to solve its problems and run the firm more efficiently, thus confirming the idea that the extension of joint regulation improves relationships with stewards. Moreover 15 per cent, in response to an open-ended question*, spontaneously mentioned helping management and/or the job to run more smoothly as the most, or among the most, satisfying aspects of their job as stewards compared with 18 per cent who saw the process of negotiation and winning concessions from management as the chief source of satisfaction. The report on that survey concludes that shop

---

* Stewards who expressed satisfaction with their jobs (81 per cent) were asked, 'In what ways?' Answers to this type of open-ended question show the relative importance or salience of different items rather than the exact proportion who subscribe to a particular point of view. Thus the importance of the 15 per cent in this context lies in its relationship to the frequency with which other items were mentioned, and indeed, the fact that it was the third most frequently mentioned item.

stewards generally act more as a lubricant in labour relations than as the irritant they are so often seen to be. (Government Social Survey, 1968)

Similarly, a survey of trade-union activists and trade-union members has shown that the trade-union activists identify more closely with the aims of the employer and are more involved in their jobs than the ordinary union members. Thus, in this case, the distinction between trade-union activists and others was not one between loyalists and disloyalists, or between supporters and opponents of the firm or between, on the other hand, 'conscious-ness' and false 'consciousness' in Marxian terms. It was more the distinction between people who become active and involved, and who identify with the organizations to which they belong, as opposed to the passive and the apathetic. The fact that the aims and interests of the two organizations to which they belong sometimes conflict they are able to sustain as readily as they can remain both good fathers and good employees despite the fact that their roles of father and employee may sometimes conflict.

Thus in one case we looked at, which involved the introduction of work measurement and job evaluation, six shop-floor repre-sentatives, one from each of the main shops involved, were nominated to monitor and participate in the evaluation and measurement carried out by the consultants employed by the firm. When the programme was complete their experience as operators and members of the work-measurement group made them particu-larly well qualified to work as job assessors. All of them accepted. On the assessment of both the convenor and management they had all been good shop-floor representatives and had become good assessors. Similarly, nearly half of the Social Survey's shop stewards expressed an interest in promotion to some kind of management position. Now, adopting a crude conflict model of the relationship between management and labour, assuming that they are on opposite and irreconcilable sides, it is easy to represent this as cynical self-seeking as illustrated by the ditty 'The working class can kiss my arse, I've got the foreman's job at last.' In fact it illustrates something quite different. It illustrates how stewards as well as employees recognize common interests as well as conflicts of interests and how they can simultaneously sustain different and apparently conflicting roles and loyalties, or rather how one role and set of loyalties will prevail in one type of circumstance and another in others.

Given this pattern of areas of conflict and areas of common interests, and the clear identification of these by many employees and trade unionists, it may seem that the traditional idea of separate channels of representation, one for negotiation through trade union representation and the other for joint consultation through elected works council, was quite logical and sensible after all.

But leaving aside all the practical weaknesses of separate channels and all the practical benefits that integration brings about, to adopt this conclusion very much over-simplifies the idea of areas of common and divergent interest. It is just not possible to categorize the different aspects of the business and employee relations and arrive at neat, self-contained discrete packages, one including topics on which there is a wide range of shared goals and ideas and the other made up of topics which usually generate differences. All topics are interrelated. Changes in one aspect often have implications for others. All have a potential for generating differences, and the same subject will sometimes be a source of difference and at others of agreement. What the recognition of both agreement and divergent interests by trade-union officers, shop stewards and workers in fact means is that the union is in principle appropriate as a single channel for accommodating both.

We have already demonstrated how this is so and how the extension of joint regulation can create a powerful medium for change in organizations where there is already full union recognition. The way full union recognition for the first time can increase rather than reduce management's scope for action is well illustrated by the case of United Biscuits.

United Biscuits is an amalgamation of a number of what were, largely, family biscuit and cake manufacturers. Thus, as a company, it inherited a very heterogeneous set of plants in terms particularly of systems of payments, wage structures and management policies. Indeed it found that within its nine original factories and among its 10,000 hourly paid employees there were 500 different jobs and rates. All were based on local traditions and practices and often bore little relationship to the jobs that people now did, the responsibilities they carried and the skills they exercised. The company consequently wanted to rationalize this situation and move towards a company payments' system common to all plants and based on systematic job evaluation. It nibbled away at this problem for some five years, making very little headway. It was then faced with a recognition strike at one of its factories which was settled on the basis of a 100 per cent membership agreement. Having conceded 100 per cent membership in one plant, there was now no reason for not extending it throughout the company. Following this, a scheme for job evaluation was jointly agreed with the unions at national level and within six months had been largely implemented throughout the company using joint shop-steward/management evaluation teams.

Thus something that had initially proved very difficult to change was relatively quickly achieved following agreement on 100 per cent membership and indeed management subsequently accepted that it would have been impossible without this: 'We would never have got off first base without full representation. We had been messing around for five years, without getting anywhere. Without anybody you could discuss it with, you did not know where to start.'

Thus the chief benefit that full union recognition had given management was a responsible body, fully representative of all relevant employees, with whom they could discuss and initiate change. The fact that now all their employees were union members, and as such had a vote, also meant that union decisions more fully reflected the views of the whole workforce instead of the vocal, active minority that had monopolized them previously. In this way full union representation enabled management to bring about change, in the same way as other companies found that the election of shop stewards and the encouragement of full union membership enabled them both to innovate and improve their employee relations. It is also important to note in this case that, once the company had conceded full recognition and membership, it went out of its way to give union representatives full facilities in order to ensure that its decisions were representative of the full membership.

The danger in not doing this is amply illustrated, again, by the STC East Kilbride case, where, as in the case of United Biscuits, the large majority of the labour force was female. Because of the difficulties women already have in doing full-time jobs as well as carrying heavier responsibilities in the home than men, it was difficult to get women elected as shop stewards. Once elected, it was difficult for them to obtain adequate training, consult their members and meet together, all outside working hours, in addition to their other responsibilities. Consequently the interests of men, the male sections and male stewards received full attention while those of women were overlooked or ignored, thus creating all kinds of sectional conflicts. This highlights again the importance of providing shop stewards with facilities for training, meeting, and consulting their members in working hours, if they are adequately and effectively to represent the interests of the whole workforce. The alternative is to leave it to the activists who are prepared to overcome all obstacles to get their interests represented. But it is a good working principle that, the more obstacles that have to be overcome to arrange a meeting the more hostile to management that meeting will eventually be.

United Biscuits set out to avoid these difficulties. They did, however, experience some local difficulties in introducing the new payments' structure. But this seemed to be largely because, although there had been a great deal of joint collaboration and management/union effort and activity at the centre, there had not been enough opportunity in the time available to involve local plant management and stewards in the design of the scheme as much as was desirable. This same pattern emerged in the early ICI MUPS difficulties at a works we visited. One of the main unions on site had taken strong objection to a package that they felt had been signed, sealed and settled at the top without taking them into account: 'From our point of view it got off right on the wrong foot. The first thing we learned was this new agreement was coming in. There was no consultation with us. There was no discussion with us. It had all been settled at national level and we had to accept it. Well we weren't having that.'

Consequently they refused to enter into discussion or negotiation for twelve months and thereafter consistently refused to be party to discussions or negotiations with a joint body including the other unions. Such difficulties are common, where both management and unions in central negotiations invest in a great deal of joint effort to arrive at an agreement for radical change which they accept will benefit all parties, only to find that those not at the centre, not involved in the design, not identified with it in the same way, are less than enthusiastic. Top management and national union leaders are then left side by side facing everybody else. This underlines how joint decision making and collaboration are required all down the line.

Equally, as we have seen, there has to be a continuous process and momentum developed in order to generate substantial and rapid change has somehow to be maintained. As United Biscuits put it: 'It is all too easy to sit back and relax after a new scheme such as this is in and working. It can begin to ossify from a very early date and become restrictive to development rather than helping it.'

In order to prevent this happening, United Bisuits has set up a working party to consider the first year's operation of the scheme and produce a report which will be jointly discussed and evaluated.

Making the union more effective as a channel of involvement

We have described at some length the changes that management needs to make and accept in order to bring about greater worker involvement in decision making. Among many other innovations, we have suggested that it needs to devolve the level of decision making more to the plant; that it needs to extend the area of joint regulation and develop institutions for that purpose; that, since the issues to be discussed are inter-related, since the body that discusses them must have effective powers, since union officers need to be brought in on as many issues as possible, not merely in those that are the subject of direct confrontation, the joint regulation should be operated through a single channel. That channel generally has to be the trade union, which should be brought more into a more co-operative, joint, problem-solving role with management on a range of topics.

But as well as demanding substantial changes in attitude and practice among many managements, such developments also make substantial demands upon unions. Not surprisingly, given that they have developed within the framework of quite different employer and management attitudes and practices, unions are often singularly ill-equipped in organization, staffing, training and objectives to meet these new demands, although where management has taken the initiative they have generally responded and accommodated to the new pattern. This only underlines the fact that changes in trade union organization, practice and attitudes do not take place in a vacuum. They occur in response to management initiatives. The general pattern is that the unions seek to make the most for their members out of the situation which management creates, whether consciously or by default. This means that union reform is dependent upon management taking the initiative in creating a situation which encourages this to come about. For instance, exhorting the unions to ensure that shop stewards are able, competent, well trained and representative is largely platitudinous unless management is prepared to provide the framework where this can come about. And we have seen that where management was seeking to make changes that demanded trained and representative shop stewards this did come about. Training was given, facilities for shop stewards provided, employees encouraged to join their union and stewards were given the opportunity to talk with them, have meetings on site, in order to make them more representative. This occurred however because management was changing its bargaining practices and institutions in ways that made these procedures relevant and appropriate.

Having made clear where the chief onus of responsibility of change lies, it is worth considering the changes that will be demanded of the unions if management does more generally take the type of initiative suggested.

Perhaps the first problems presented by our prescription, as it affects the unions, are the two inter-related ones that often unions do not want to participate in joint problem solving and the union is often not seen as a channel of involvement by workers. As we have been at pains to demonstrate, what might appear to be reluctance to collaborate and a tendency to adopt a purely opposition role is more often just a reflection of lack of opportunity and management's casting the union purely in the role of opposition. At the same time, as mentioned in our reservations about the scope of total involvement exercises, it is sometimes more than that. Trade unionists have been reluctant to become involved in the drawing-up of plans for change, the definition of criteria for job evaluation, or the joint evaluation of jobs. They have feared that they would become too committed to the changes or the decisions in advance and would be less able to defend and promote their members' interests subsequently. They would have weakened their case for demanding the highest price for the change, or they would be in a weaker position to pursue members' grievances about their job evaluation if they or their colleagues had been involved in the process.

In adopting this view they have been supported by those scholars who have argued that the basis of industrial democracy, and the chief scope for worker involvement in decision making, lie in the power of the trade union to challenge and oppose management. They argue that anything which reduces the unions' power to oppose, decreases industrial democracy, and hence involvement in management decisions creates the illusion of involvement while reducing the substance. (Clegg, 1960)

We have accepted all along, indeed have strongly promoted, the idea that effective worker involvement in decision making is dependent on workers being members of strong, representative trade unions, and also on the union being the chief channel of involvement and able to oppose where it sees the interests of its members threatened. But no one body that seeks only to oppose can be fully representative of the interests of workers, who see a wide area of common interests with management as well as differing ones. Indeed we would suggest that part of the reason for workers' apathy or opposition to their union, their reluctance to see it as a channel of involvement, lies in the way that all it does is oppose. Moreover it would be possible to have full industrial democracy in the 'opposition' sense without any worker having any feeling that he had played any part in decisions. He could be well represented at local, district and national levels by strong, well-informed union officers who promoted and defended his interests, as they saw them, by challenging and opposing management without his feeling he had any part in influencing events. Indeed we would suggest that often this is the situation that currently prevails and if it is, then according to the 'opposition' thesis the industrial worker has often had industrial democracy all his life without knowing it. But our reading of the current situation is that industrial democracy requires more than this.

Increasingly, workers want a direct say in events and are not content to be represented at some lofty level by someone pursuing what he assumes to be their interests though not accountable to them. This will require direct involvement in decision making, and collaboration on a wide range of decisions as well as opposition. It is more desirable that better, more acceptable decisions are reached through this means, than that decisions are resisted purely because they have been unilaterally reached by management or because they are inferior through not having had any input of workers' ideas. This is desirable with regard both to the smooth running of business and effective worker involvement in decision making. Thus, if we take the example of job evaluation again, it is better that a system is devised that gives rise to fewer grievances because it has been jointly developed and is based upon shared ideas and values about how different groups should be remunerated, than that workers' representatives remain aloof in order to be able to pursue uninhibitedly the larger number of grievances that will arise from a unilaterally designed management scheme. It is true that worker representative involvement in the design and development process has its dangers, chief of which is the danger of the representative becoming isolated from the group he represents. This only underlines the importance of management creating the framework within which representatives can maintain contact with those they represent, to whom, of course, they are ultimately accountable through the electoral system.

The antithesis to the 'opposition through the union' concept of industrial democracy is the 'participative, consultative style of management' concept. This derives from the human relations or socio-psychological approaches we identified as being associated with writers such as McGregor, Likert, Argyris and Herzberg. They argue that the worker's need for involvement can be satisfied by increasing his scope for autonomy and self-expression on the job, by job enrichment and by developing participative, consultative, democratic styles of supervision and management, within which the immediate superior will be 'employee oriented' and 'supportive'. Employee attitude surveys can also facilitate such results. The chief criticism that has been levelled against this concept is that where employers have sought to implement it they have done so in order to give workers the illusion of involvement without the reality of power. Such employers, it is alleged, have sought to assuage the rising demand among workers to have a say in events through these means, while maintaining the existing power structure and their own freedom of unilateral decision making. In particular they have tried, through democratic styles of management, to deflect workers from the unionization that would give them a 'real' say by being able to challenge management and thereby effectively change the power structure. But, in so far as this has happened, then it could be replied that the desire to avoid unionization has made such employers actually modify the power structure. It may well be that at one end of the spectrum that has underlain our analysis throughout, this is an appropriate medium for worker involvement. But it has to be added that the number of British companies where anything approaching this has been brought about could be numbered on the fingers of one mutilated hand. Equally, at the opposite end of the spectrum, it may be appropriate that the pure concept of opposition through the union is the most appropriate and we have no illusions that there are no employers who discount the interest of employees in decision making or who will continue to resist the need for the extension of joint regulation. But ideally we conclude that effective worker involvement in decision making requires strong representation at all levels of decision making, including the scope to oppose. There must also be direct involvement at the workplace including both collaboration and opposition. Within this framework, as we have seen, there is plenty of scope for the media of involvement, provided by the 'human relations' approach under the over-all umbrella of joint regulation, with the union effectively the single channel of involvement.

The second main problem with this, however, is that often the union is not seen as a channel of involvement by employees. First, it is often seen as a means of insurance or protection, so that however fair and good they think their employer is, in the last analysis, should they be injured, disciplined, dismissed or involved in any dispute with the employer, they have a powerful body to back and support them. Secondly, the union is often seen as a means of increasing earnings or material rewards and workers are 'subsequently only involved in their unions to the extent that those organizations protect and increase those material rewards.' (Goldthorpe *et al.*, 1969) Thirdly, the union is often seen simply in terms of traditional loyalties — 'a good working man is a trade unionist' — but rarely explicitly as a channel of involvement and indeed it may even be rejected as such. (Goldthorpe *et al.*, ibid)

Our interpretation is not that the possibility of the union becoming an effective channel of involvement is excluded because that is not what workers want of it, but that it is a reflection of two quite different phenomena. First it is a reflection partly of the reality of the situation. Workers expect union action in only very limited areas because their experience of union policy and practice has led them to expect this. Employers' traditional reluctance to see an extension of joint regulation has confined union activity to these areas and the trade-union movement has been too willing to confine the scope of its activities. It has limited its effort on the industrial front to narrow economic goals, to the distribution of wealth created by industry and hence improving wages, hours and conditions. It has looked to the political arm of the labour movement to bring about changes in the distribution of power, ushering in industrial democracy through public ownership. It should now be clear that that has proved a blind alley, that ownership is often irrelevant to effective worker involvement in decision making of the type we have been discussing, and that trade unions are increasingly going to need to concern themselves with these matters if they are going to satisfy the rising demands of their members.

But as well as reflecting the situation as it is, the tendency for workers to look to the union for limited benefits also partly reflects a difference between their definition of what the union is, and our own. There is a tendency for workers to see the union as some distinct entity outside, separate from what they and their representatives do and achieve at work in the plant, despite the fact that they are union members and their plant representatives are in fact union officers. Thus, although we have argued the need for a range of opportunities for involvement within the plant, within a single channel of union representation, the results and effects of this will not necessarily be attributed by workers to the union. In fact they will feel that they themselves have brought these changes about rather than some separate, outside body. Indeed to satisfy the demand for involvement it is necessary that they should feel that it is their achievement, while, for all the reasons cited, it is equally important that in effect, if not in perception, this should come within the framework of union representation. At the same time if the union, meaning the national leadership, full-time officers and bureaucracy, wishes to increase its standing with its members, then in both its public utterances and general policies it should seek to create a framework and climate that encourages this to come about. To date the leadership within individual unions has often been slow to react to the changing situation whereby to many workers 'the shop steward is the union' and this has reinforced the feeling that the union is irrelevant to the needs they have at work. Moreover the structure and development of the union movement as a whole does not lend itself happily to a plant-bargaining situation. We have seen the development of plant bargaining as a prerequisite of effective worker involvement in decision making. Others have argued that it is equally important for bringing back order and control, through shared control, into workplace labour relations. But each of these objectives requires major changes in the over-all direction of the union movement. For the unions at the centre and the top we see the major switch in emphasis and direction as a move away from seeking to change their own relationships with employers towards one of unions allowing and assisting their members to reconstruct their relationships with employers along the more equitable and constructive lines advocated in earlier chapters. This change of emphasis will in turn demand radical changes in organization. Plant bargaining for instance, which is central to the change, puts an enormous strain on a union's resources if it is going to service all its members adequately. Moreover this strain highlights one of the chief institutional obstacles to effective plant bargaining, that of multi-unionism, for clearly a multiplicity of unions covering similar work groups within one plant is a severe waste of resources. As most unions even now find themselves over-stretched, they could not possibly hope to give participating work groups the servicing and support they need.

Thus one of the first requirements for appropriate new institutions is a strategy for overcoming the problems of multi-unionism. We have tended so far to neglect this difficulty by talking of 'the union' as a channel of involvement and have ignored the existence of a number of different unions in most workplaces. In fact the gradual breakdown of multi-unionism through amalgamations and greater inter-union co-operation at plant and company level has been increasingly coming about and is likely to continue as part of the natural evolution of the union movement. It needs to be accelerated in order to cope with the changes we foresee.

The Government's 1968 Social Survey of Workplace Industrial Relations showed that 82 per cent of stewards said they had more than one union representing manual workers in their plant but only 31 per cent had more than one union competing for workers on the same grade. The pace of amalgamations has certainly not slackened since that report was produced hence the problem should, slowly, become less significant. Of more interest however are the figures which show that 50 per cent of stewards think that fewer unions would be helpful while only 8 per cent think they would not. Similarly 80 per cent of union officers thought their position would be aided by fewer unions but conversely only 42 per cent of works managers and 49 per cent of personnel officers thought this would be helpful. What is interesting about these figures is that multi-unionism and its accompanying demarcation problems have always been emphasized as a limitation on management action and change, whereas these figures suggest it is more of a drawback to union officials.

Certainly the continuation of multi-unionism operates quite as much against the interests of workers as of management. It tends to concentrate attention on wage differentials and financial matters to the exclusion of other areas, generating friction between work groups, fragmentation and disunity. Moreover in those situations where there is more than one union within a work group it may tend to encourage parallel organizations, such as non-union, elected works' councils, to grow up and will certainly make exercises in involvement at work more complicated. On the other hand, it may help to institutionalize an inevitable conflict such as the classic situation we have encountered where a new factory in a semi-rural area has a workforce split into one half made up of long-standing locals and the other of overspills from a city. Yet, even in this situation, multi-unionism may only serve to prolong a conflict.

Assuming however that amalgamations can be seen only as a very long-term solution, a first step to solve this problem should be the full recognition of the existence and necessity of joint committees at plant level, of the type that was common in the change programmes we have described. Beyond that, it has been suggested, exchanges of members or rather of membership rights should be encouraged. (Paynter, 1970) Dual membership might be the least painful way of developing this. In the white-collar area particularly it should be possible to prevent a free for all.

It is extremely important, in relation to the changes mentioned above, that competition for members should be even more effectively controlled than it is at present by the Bridlington Rules. Although it may appear that by restricting competition for members the unions limit individual choice, it is in precisely this apparently monopolistic situation that union democracy can best thrive.

This brings us back to the second and perhaps less straightforward area in which reform is imperative, namely the internal structure and representative nature of individual unions. At present, union leaders are usually loath to allow any opposition to emerge within their organizations and certainly the idea of an institutionalized opposition is, not surprisingly, totally rejected. In a situation where a union was no longer fearful of its members either forming a breakaway union or, as happened at Ford's Halewood plant, switching from one union to another, then opposition could be accommodated much more easily. There might be doubts that certain union leaders would still try to retain a semi-authoritarian structure and certainly it is remarkable how, at present, the philosophy of each of the major unions so clearly reflects the views of a few men at the top. However, it is not surprising that representative democracy does not work in the present union structure where the most likely action of the dissatisfied is to opt out of the system altogether. Obviously there will be fears that the existence of opposition groups will reduce efficiency but the opposing faction would accept certain rules and ends like any other group working within a democratic system. There is a basis for such opposition in the general unions through the existence of different trade groups whose interests might clash, and there is certainly a case for allowing such groups to openly discuss and resolve differences through union channels. The degree to which these autonomous trade groups might be able to exist in the large unions has not yet been fully explored but, if such a move were successful, it would go beyond Donovan's fairly far-reaching recommendation which we quoted earlier. Perhaps more crucially, the belief that the unions represent their members' wishes fairly accurately and efficiently is based on the belief that the leaders and full-time officials know and can reflect the wishes of their members properly. We have found cases, on the one hand, where this has clearly not happened and there has been deep-rooted disagreement with the policy followed by the union; but even more significantly there have been a large number of cases where the members have been fairly happy with their wages but other sources of dissatisfaction grew up simply because union officials never came to the plant to take action.

The development of democratic institutions, however, can only conceivably come about in reaction to an already changed situation. The impetus could well be provided by the growth of plant bargaining. This has accelerated in the last five years or so, partly in response to the development of types of collective bargaining more suited to plant-level negotiations (such as productivity agreements and the change programmes we have quoted) and partly as a result of desire for greater involvement from active trade unionists on the shop floor. In addition, Donovan's recommendations produced a favourable climate, which was subsequently reinforced by the incomes policy (our study of productivity cases showed that for nearly half of the sample this was the first plant agreement) and finally the pressure of work on full-time officials has continued to grow. This has meant that many shop stewards have been given leading roles in negotiations where formerly their contribution was fairly minor. Our studies have shown that while many coped quite adequately with the new demands, others found themselves completely at sea in their first experience of this role. Normally such feelings of inadequacy did not last beyond the first round of negotiations but many still feel very disadvantaged by the lack of information and expert advice. This feeling has been extended to a full-time officer in one case where a small union had an officer whose area was so wide that the steward felt he could not stand up as an equal to top-management negotiators whatever his ability. This may seem to put management very much at an advantage, for the idea of being able to put over, on an inexperienced shop steward, what would not get past experienced, full-time officers might have a certain attraction for some managers. Lest they be tempted, we should point out that we found more than one case where a first productivity deal gave management a great deal of change for a very small cost but the long-term result was greatly increased resistance to change or at least a considerably more aggressive approach.

For instance, we found one case where stewards had signed a three-year agreement, part of which involved giving up entitlement to sickness pay for a 2½p-an-hour increase. Management tried the same proposal on supervisors with no success – as the personnel manager explained 'Your average supervisor is brighter and thinks a bit further ahead than your average man on the shop-floor.' They found, however, that although the men kept to the agreement, when it came up for renewal they put forward a memorandum with thirty new demands and were in no mood to be conciliatory.

What is needed, clearly, is the type of training and facilities that were provided in the major change programmes we cited, together with a management awareness that there are no longer-term advantages in trying to exploit a short-term period of inexperience. Back-up servicing is also needed.

This underlines the two related problems with which unions will have to deal in making themselves more effective channels of involvement. The first of these is the range and quality of the services provided by the union for its members, and the second, the state of decision making at shop-floor level. As far as the first is concerned there are a number of specific areas, for example, availability of information and communications generally, training of shop stewards and research and technical services, where improvement is important. (Hughes, 1968) As far as training stewards to take charge of negotiations over the whole range of decision making is concerned, the 1968 Social Survey found that only 30 per cent of stewards from six major unions had taken part in a training course, with the figures ranging from 67 per cent of NUR stewards to 18 per cent of AUBTW and 22 per cent of NUGMW. There is no doubt that these training facilities are being expanded rapidly but the problem will have to be given high priority if stewards are to be asked to cover topics which have, in the past, been peripheral to their main tasks. (Cmnd. 4668, 1971)

The problem of communications and availability of information is more complicated and to some extent a matter of formal communications, such as union journals and the possibility of their development into at least semi-independent organs, carrying comment and news. Also important is the new development which we saw in 1971 with the publication of the T & GWU's Ford Wage Claim which, in its size, scope and availability surpassed anything that had gone before. (T & GWU, 1971)

In this context it is interesting that we were talking to a group of shop stewards at an ICI plant shortly after the publication of the equally prestigious and impressive claim made by their national officers to ICI. The first that they had heard of its contents was through the press and television and they had still had no direct communication about it through official union channels. This issue unleashed a catalogue of grievances to the effect that questions sent to union officers were not being answered and information was not being received. It is clear that, beyond the formal channels for the flow of information, it is as important for the unions to develop effective communication with their members and officers as it is for management to communicate with their employees. However bad management may have been on this score, the unions have almost certainly been worse. But without communication involvement at shop-floor level is a pipe dream and the flaring up of insurgent, shop-floor feeling as at Pilkingtons in 1970 is much more likely. Moreover our studies suggest that cases like Pilkingtons represent just the tip of an iceberg in which the more normal response is apathy and disillusionment with the union.

The solution to this question of availability of information will not be wholly solved by spending more on services. The increasing size and scope of research and technical services is certainly necessary for we have found a number of cases, particularly when complex problems concerning international finance are concerned, in which even the full-time officials simply did not have the expertise to represent their members adequately. For example, in one such case in Wales, the firm had offered to 'open the books' but the offer had been on the table for five years because neither the permanent officials nor the shop stewards had the necessary expertise. Moreover however large such services become, they can never do more than give support to members operating at local level. It is therefore at this level that the most important developments must take place. This brings us back to the state of decision making on the shop floor.

Whether or not a radical development in joint regulation comes about, it is quite clear that there has been an irreversible shift of influence towards the shop steward – partly a result of plant bargaining. If there is to be a growth in structured work groups involved in decision making then this shift of influence must be recognized and formalized. In the first place, two inter-related problems must be dealt with by the unions: the relationship between branch activities and shop activities; and the role of union officials in relation to shop stewards. As far as the branch is concerned, the 1968 Social Survey found that 63 per cent of unionists do not belong to plant-based branches. In view of the fact that, for a very large number of unionists, the only really relevant union activity takes place at their own workplace, this is clearly an anomaly. It is true that decisions regarding a particular plant are, in practice, often more likely to be taken at that plant, but time and again we found that decisions on crucial elements of the major change programmes cited were delayed by branch or district committees upon which no one from the plant was represented. Sometimes the decisions were in defiance of the wishes of plant officers and workers. Clearly where decisions are taken *de facto*, at the plant, this should be recognized in the formal structure and put into effect.

With regard to the position of the full-time official, the distinction between his nominal and practical powers has been generally recognized, and has indeed been recently acknowledged by the TUC, which has set up a major enquiry into the position of local officials. The degree of formal power held by the district official differs within individual unions but in most the actual power and influence of the officers greatly exceed those of their rule books. There are a number of reasons for this, the most obvious is that the local official is the man with the most expertise and knowledge. This is gradually becoming a less overwhelming reason as training for stewards becomes more widespread. Clearly, it would be desirable for the power of district officials to coincide more closely with the limitations imposed by the rules of many unions but it is equally true that the needs of efficiency have to be satisfied as well as those of democracy. It is certain that an effective system of joint regulation at plant level would necessarily reduce the power of the district officials. One of the reasons why such officials have in the past been allowed to exceed their prescribed powers has been that only a very small minority of members have been active enough to challenge their authority if differences arose. This raises again the branch-shop dichotomy, and the shift of decision making from branch to plant and the involvement of the workforce in that decision-making process would leave the full-time official less able to exert direct power.

Certain unions, notably the T & GWU, encourage stewards and members to assert themselves *vis-á-vis* their full-time officials. However, there is still a strong tendency in many unions for the official to continue to lead the negotiating team and to have more-or-less formal power over a wide area. The dangers of too large a work load have been fully documented but, quite apart from this, it is somewhat illogical to set up plant bargaining and then have it led from outside.

Our study of productivity deals clearly showed that often the most unsatisfactory agreements from all points of view were those in which the full-time union officer had played the leading part in design and negotiation, leaving the stewards with either a very subsidiary role, or none at all. Thus, in one case, management and full-time officers completed a very amicable agreement only for both parties to be astonished a few weeks later when stewards, for the first time ever, slammed in a demand on their own for a 14 per cent wage increase.

It is then at this level that structural changes must occur for reasons of both union democracy and efficiency. As Roberts found, one of union officials' main grievances is the sense of insecurity felt by those who have to seek re-election. (Roberts, 1956) Yet if officials were to retain the power that they have in some unions, there would be a strong case for making them more accountable to their members. We have come across the problem that many union officers are loath to let us speak to their stewards, though they are happy to speak to us themselves. There are a number of possible reasons for this but, at best, it seems likely to mean that the officer believes the steward to be less articulate or more ingenuous than himself and, at worst, that there is considerable disagreement between officer and steward. However, this problem should not exist if decision making moves to the plant. The role of the union officer would change radically more towards that of a servicing agent. He would clearly retain a good deal of influence but very little direct power. He would make sure that local deals adhered broadly to union policy and would provide the representatives at plant level with the sort of expert and technical assistance that would undoubtedly be needed. Detailed changes in, for instance, responsibility for membership, which would allow stewards some form of direct contact with hierarchy and presence at negotiations, should be very much a question for each organization to decide.

These changes will for some unions be more a shift in emphasis than a radical change of direction. The process whereby the balance of power has shifted to the shop floor is already far advanced in some sectors of industry. As with the change to plant-based organizational units however, what is needed is a more formal recognition of this process. Such recognition would allow union officials the security of tenure which they could have in other jobs without the risk of accusation that their role is undemocratic. The importance of security of tenure should not be underestimated because without it, even in the present circumstances, it is likely to be difficult to get top-class representatives and, certainly in the situation we are visualizing, it would put a heavy strain on union resources if the man they had just spent a considerable amount of money on training was likely to be removed at the next elections.

At present, decision making in the unions is decided as much by organizational as by social and economic pressures. The national, regional, and plant-level decision makers correspond to some extent to levels of decision making within the firm; but the same is not true of the local official, whose position is based on the ideal of a workforce united by common ideals and not just by the fact that the members share the same place of work. This ideal is certainly worthy of retention, but should not be allowed to obscure the fact that the units are often so large as to make it unmanageable, and it is to some extent mythical in any case. By reassessing this position it is quite possible for unions to increase democracy and efficiency at the same time.

The first thing to overcome in bringing about these changes is the suspicion felt by many trade unionists of anything that smacks of collaboration with management as opposed to negotiation. While the independence of the unions is a delicate matter, it is hardly consistent with our involvement case studies to suggest that union members or officials would be less independent because they were involved in taking decisions which affected their jobs. The central point which we have already made earlier is that workers remain independent as long as they make decisions through their own organizations rather than have them imposed from outside.

The grass-roots changes that will be most difficult to bring about, however, are those which will affect the power and accountability of the union hierarchies. We have already mentioned the formal trappings of democracy (independent journals, opportunities for opposition etc) which we would hope to see develop in the long term, but more immediately the formal granting of considerable autonomy for groups of members at plant level would, in most cases, change their relationship with those at regional and national level and be likely to have a radical effect on union organizations and policy.

We do not advocate a total change in union decision making, however. Clearly management will continue to take decisions at plant, company and national level and so must the unions. This is particularly true of the level of basic wages, but beyond that many more decisions about supplementary payments and conditions of work must be taken at plant level.

We have stressed elsewhere that we do not believe it possible to produce a set of directives which are equally appropriate to all situations and the same applies here. In the first place, for some unions our proposals will involve not much more than a more positive recognition of, and reaction to, developments which have already had some effect. Thus those unions that have already institutionalized the position of their shop stewards to some extent and have given them considerable autonomy will not need to bring about any radical changes in attitude within their organizations. They will, however, have greatly to increase their efficiency. This means improvement of services but, far more importantly, it is quite pointless to replace fairly close control by union officials with no contact at all between them and the shop-floor representatives. Clearly some less advanced sectors of industry will still need very close supervision by full-time officers and there is probably a case for a gradual change-over in the roles of the officers, with an initial division of labour between those who fulfil the new servicing function and those who perform the traditional negotiating role.

These changes are mainly structural and although they are expensive in time and money do not really involve any radical change of direction. For some unions, however, the decentralization process may be far more painful. These are the unions which are heavily centralized with a considerable measure of formal power resting with the officers. Such unions will obviously not make radical changes without good reason. There will, however, be some organizational pressure if plant bargaining continues to grow and social pressure if such institutions as joint shop stewards' committees develop on the shop floor. This would be a long, slow process however and can be quickened only by pressure for change coming from management and shop floor together deciding a programme of greater involvement, advantageous to both.

The way in which trade unions will become more effective channels of involvement therefore varies considerably. For a union like the NUM or the NUR the problems are largely internal. The NUM branch official is based on a colliery in any case so the problem of branch *versus* shop floor does not arise. However, the area officials are very powerful, negotiations have until recently been very centralized and, even though the branch is based on the workplace, there is no indication that it has any better attendance figures. Nonetheless the NCB have been carrying out some fairly advanced involvement exercises on a mainly consultative basis with face teams and these experiments might well form a basis for the extension of joint regulation through involvement with the union looking into the question of how much autonomy lay members could be allowed. (Shephard, 1970) Clearly the union would want all major decisions to be passed through for confirmation, but with this carried out, and with the advice of local officials, there seems no reason why union policy should not retain its coherence.

For the general unions the problems are made more complex because accommodation has to be reached with other organizations.

We have already mentioned the growth of joint shop-stewards' committees. We welcome this development as long as the unions themselves recognize its advantages and give formal recognition. Generally, however, while we have advocated particular ends, we do not feel we can encourage specific methods of reaching those ends. The means will depend on the number of shop stewards who have had training, the ratio of officials to members, the number of unions in a plant, the amount of autonomy lay representatives have had in the past and other variables. In certain plants it is certainly feasible to encourage the workforce to participate in involvement exercises now, but in others, considerable work in training, education and breaking down suspicion between trades is needed. In addition, all the unions will have to look to their rule books, which may need to be much more flexible if changes in branch organization and workplace autonomy are to be realized.

8 Workers' Directors

Possibly the aspect of workers' involvement in decision making which, on the one hand, has the most dramatic and superficial appeal and, on the other, raises the most unreasonable and ill-founded fears is that of involvement at the highest level in the enterprise: the board room. Supporters of this idea see it as a means of both establishing and demonstrating a greater degree of harmony in the enterprise. Given the multiplicity of the interests that the enterprise serves, it is suggested that the involvement of workers' representatives in the formulation of objectives and policy at board level will lead to improved decision making. Workers' ideas and interests will be fed in at a stage when they can be balanced against other interests and reconciled with these, rather than companies formulating policies oblivious of, or in defiance of, workers' interests and with resultant opposition to the proposals, resolved only through conflict. Moreover, it is argued, the existence of workers' directors will give workers a greater sense of being part of the enterprise. They will identify more with the enterprise and its goals, feeling that it is being governed by a body within which they have representatives, rather than a body composed of people whose sole function and obligation is to serve a group whose interests are often in conflict with their own: the shareholders. Through the medium of worker representation on the board it is suggested that the decisions taken by the board will, in fact and appearance, be more in line with workers' interests and ideas, and therefore more acceptable.

These arguments are, however, subject to sharp criticism from representatives both of organized labour, and of capital or share-holders. From the left it is argued once again, as with trade-union collaboration in decision making at lower levels, that such innova-

139

tions would give the illusion of greater worker involvement while reducing the substance. As long as ownership rests in private hands, workers could never hope to achieve as much effective power through representation on the board as they can achieve through their collective power, set in opposition to the interests of management as shareholders' representatives. Thus not only would the creation of workers' directors not substantially increase their involvement in decision making, but it would in practice decrease it. It would create yet another channel of worker representation separate from the union, thereby reducing the status and importance of that body. It would make workers less conscious that fundamentally their interests are in conflict with those of the enterprise, thus again weakening their attachment to the union. For these reasons, critics see the idea of workers' directors as yet another manipulative management ploy designed to kid workers that their interests are being fully served and are perfectly congruent with those of the enterprise. At the same time, the trade union, as the only effective medium for serving workers' interests, is weakened.

Were this the case then it might be expected that the most enthusiastic supporters of the concept of workers' directors would come from the ranks of the representatives and spokesmen of capital and shareholding interests. It is a matter of observation that this is not the case. In the main they are far from enthusiastic. Indeed it would not unduly caricature their position to suggest that they are usually content to take the view that there is no real conflict between the interests of shareholders and workers, that management accountable to the shareholder is quite capable of taking decisions in everybody's interests and that only politically motivated trouble-makers would pretend otherwise. In addition the absolute objection on principle is sometimes voiced that any provision for employee directors attacks property rights. This, however, seems to be the type of misconception of the rights conferred by the ownership of property that we considered in dealing with the question of management prerogatives in Chapter Seven.

It will be quite clear, from the account and analysis of procedures and institutions for enhanced worker involvement in decision making in the preceding chapters, that the appointment of workers' directors on its own is not going to usher in a new order of relationship between the worker and the enterprise overnight. It will not automatically ensure that conflicts of interest disappear, that workers will see their interests fully and adequately represented in board decisions and that they will feel more involved in the enterprise through indirectly contributing to its decision making at the highest level. Indeed as far as any feeling on the part of workers that they are influencing events is concerned, our analysis indicates that representation on the board is likely to be the least important channel of involvement. This, however, leaves open the question as to whether the appointment of workers' directors would add a further dimension, contributing something extra to all the other media for involvement that we have described, or whether it would detract from the effectiveness of the other media.

Answering these questions in terms of British society is made particularly difficult by the fact that, within the mainstream of both public and private industry and business, there is only one enterprise that has appointed workers' directors as such. Other countries, however, have had a richer experience and this may provide some clues as to the likely effects here. Particularly pertinent is the experience of Germany with its two-tier board system.

In 1951 legislation was introduced under which supervisory boards comprising eleven members, five from management, five from the trade unions and one neutral, were to control the over-all policy of enterprise in the German coal and steel industries. A year later, in 1952, similar legislation was extended to the rest of German industry, but in this case companies were obliged to have only one-third of the supervisory boards made up by trade-union members. Perhaps the main task of these boards was to elect an actual executive board consisting of three members: commercial, technical and labour directors. The labour director in the coal and steel industries is elected only by the union representatives on the supervisory board and is directly responsible to them. This structure is then supported at grass-roots level by the statutory provision for works councils on which workers are directly represented. These councils were given broad statutory authority in certain areas but in practice this has tended to be confined to the right to be consulted · about matters arising in such areas.

In terms of evaluating the effects of workers' directors this package presents some problems because it has three distinct components' the workers' representatives on the supervisory board, the labour director appointed by the supervisory board, and the statutory works' council. Apart from difficulties inherent in distinguishing between the contributions of different components of the package, opinion is divided over the effects of the total package. Indeed it is notable how such opinion tends to be very much in line with the starting point of those who express it. Fogarty argues there is evidence of greater responsibility and a more positive interest from the workers and a more human approach to such problems as redundancy from management. (Fogarty, 1968)

Dahrendorf, however, shows conclusively that the changes have not led to any great worker awareness or feeling that they are determining or even influencing events. Blumenthal suggests, moreover, that any change in management policy and practice and the consequent benefits to workers are attributable more to the existence of a union-controlled labour director than directly to the supervisory board members. (Blumenthal, 1956) He also highlights how supervisory boards have tended to develop an informal division of function, within which the union representatives confined their attention to pay structures and conditions of employment while leaving other areas of decision making to management. There is no evidence that coal and steel workers, who had half their supervisory board made up of union representatives, received any greater increases in earnings as a result than did those workers in industries where one-third of the supervisory board is appointed by unions. This may allay the fears of management that the appointment of workers' directors would contribute to accelerated wage-push inflation, more than it will create disillusionment among supporters of the concept. There is some evidence that the trade unions fear that the total package would weaken unions at plant level had some substance, but this is almost certainly more attributable to the growth of the works' councils and their representatives being given a greater say over areas where workers could have exerted considerable power anyway, through the normal processes of voluntary, collective bargaining. Moreover union representatives have tended to become more identified with management. Though a more benevolent approach has been developed, the system, while it gives full representation, no more generates greater involvement in decision making at work than has joint consultation in the UK. Some commentators like Clegg go further and suggest that German managers have used co-determination as a means of reducing the influence of unions inside the factory by increasing employees' identification with the firm. Finally while there is evidence that day-to-day relations are less formal, wage negotiations appeared comparatively unaffected.

The German example is to some extent unique in that it was the first example of privately owned industry being required by law to accept any employee representatives on their boards, and to accept a substantial proportion. The other interesting examples of boardroom participation on a large scale have differed from Germany either because the industry involved is nationalized, or, alternatively, because workers' control in terms of financial ownership already existed. This is the case in Israel, for example.

The Israeli situation is a complicated one, with the trade-union movement owning industrial enterprises but having them run by professional managers; this traditionally has meant that they have differed from the normal joint stock companies only in so far as the unions have been the stock holders rather than private individuals or financial institutions. Indeed normal conflicts have been heightened by the existence of separate, diverse and often competing immigrant groups within the organization. On the other hand, there is a larger degree of ideological commitment to the goals of the enterprise than one might expect to find elsewhere.

Despite high commitment to the idea of worker participation, initiatives in the direction of greater worker involvement in decision making within the *Histadruth* enterprises have tended to fade and die if, in fact, they did not fail to get off the ground at all. (Tabb and Goldfarb, 1969) The reasons for these failures are clear. For while there was a general belief in the desirability of participation among all sections of the enterprise, there was very little idea of what form it should take. There was the tendency to assume that because the trade unions owned the companies this meant that any conflicts could be resolved simply by good intentions. Secondly, the changes were initiated by the central *Histadruth* hierarchy without any real attempt to involve local managers, trade unionists or workers in the design or setting up of the institutions for participation. Thirdly, and consequently, neither the objectives of the schemes, nor the authority and function of the works' councils or the roles of the participants were ever clearly agreed or defined. Indeed the councils established generally took much the same form as joint consultative bodies in the UK and proved to have all the same inadequacies that we have described.

The example of Yugoslavia, whose experiments with worker

self-management have been given the widest publicity of all in the last decade, is more encouraging. The Yugoslavs specifically identified the rights of ownership as crucial and attempted to deal with these by stating in the self-management laws of 1960 that an enterprise is public property, managed for the people by those who work in it. In this situation, where the unions had no real opposition role, they eventually tended to be by-passed and, as their direct influence waned, they often became mainly educative organizations. This did not give rise to manifest difficulties in times of economic expansion but the growing unemployment of the 1960s put considerable strain on the system as the needs of the enterprise and the short-term needs of the workers clashed more often. This was made more acute because the self-management laws conceived of the enterprise as a closed unit and therefore did not take into account the possibility of conflicts arising out of competition. Conflicts became more frequent with the continuing decentralizing of the economy. Moreover, as enterprises rationalized and as decision making grew more remote, there was a tendency to transfer the workers' power of self-management to committees not directly elected by the workers, particularly when enterprises were in trouble. In these cases, because the role of the union had been unsurped by that of the self-management committees, there was no one to represent the specific views of the workers as opposed to the needs of the enterprise in any given situation.

To the generally disappointing picture emerging within privately owned enterprises can be added the Norwegian experience of co-determination, subject of a study by the Tavistock Institute, the findings of which demonstrated how workers' directors found it difficult if not impossible to reconcile their functions as both board members and representatives of the workforce. They therefore tended to grow more and more remote from the groups who had elected them.

It is notable in all these cases that the greatest disillusionment with the idea of worker representation on boards is often being expressed by the same idealists who initially had been the most enthusiastic supporters of the concept. In Germany, liberal social democrats and representatives of organized labour both entered into the initiatives with the highest hopes but were often disappointed by the results. However, the law was strengthened towards the end of 1971 in a way designed to give works' councils greater powers and it remains to be seen what effect this will have.

The Yugoslav system has been the object of many hopes and expectations among those genuinely interested in industrial democracy. Failure to achieve perfection has only made disappointment greater. Yet, given our analysis of the basic requirements of worker involvement in decision making, it is not at all surprising that so many of these attempts to establish industrial democracy through the governing body of the enterprise have failed to live up to expectations. We have shown how industrial democracy needs to be built from the bottom upwards: how the starting point must be the extension of worker influence on decisions about day-to-day activities at the workplace; how this requires the delegation and decentralization of decision making and how effective worker involvement in decision making normally requires membership of strong collectivities, independent of the enterprise, and through which employees can challenge management decision making as well as co-operate in joint decision making. Clearly, ensuring that there are workers' representatives at the highest level of decision making does not, on its own, contribute to any of these basic requirements. It is possible to give convincing explanations why the different systems we have looked at have proved disappointing without discarding the idea of workers' directors completely. They did not for example, provide an effective infrastructure to the functions and roles of workers' directors, but this does not mean that they have no useful purpose to play.

In Germany a potentially far-reaching reform has had far less effect than had been hoped and we would contend that this is largely because there was never a realistic attempt to relate that reform to the position of the union member on the shop floor. Certainly there are also works' councils but the main effect is simply to create organizations parallel to the trade unions which has left both types of institution weaker than they might have been at the workplace. There was not, therefore, and still is not, an adequate democratic base which involves the mass of the members in the co-determination system. Similarly, in the more limited Norwegian case, the workers' directors are few in number and have no real strength.

The Israeli situation also was remarkable for the lack of involvement of the ordinary worker and union officer and of local management. This in itself gave the initiatives no chance of success.

As Blumberg (1968) says the basic fault of these schemes has been the failure 'to change the meaning of work for the worker'. Yet it should be noted that Tabb and Goldfarb point to a very large majority of shop stewards still enthusiastic about workers' participation, and there is certainly no suggestion that the German workers would allow co-determination to disappear.

Yugoslavia is rather a different case as it has genuinely attempted to democratize the work situation and there are few who would not agree that there has been qualified success throughout the economy and considerable success in individual enterprises. However, the Yugoslavs did not fully recognize the sorts of conflicts that can grow within an industrial enterprise and therefore did not provide any institutional basis for an opposition should the need arise. As we have made clear, it is normally a prerequisite for effective worker involvement that the workforce should have a strong organization which does not depend on that firm for its existence if workers' interests are to be fully represented.

In applying the lessons of these systems to our own experience two things are worth noting. The first is that our experiments in this field are insignificant compared with the four countries we have noted, not to mention others such as France, Sweden or India. Secondly, it is abundantly clear that employee representation at board level does not automatically increase most workers' feelings of involvement.

It is interesting in this context that a Gallup survey in 1969 found that, although there was a large majority of workers in favour of participating at board level, 48 per cent thought it would have no effect on them whatsoever. Possibly the clearest case of this is the present experiment with workers' directors in the British Steel Corporation. It is very difficult to see how the present experiments or even greatly extended versions can possibly increase the sense of involvement to any significant degree. However, the Corporation is clearly not attempting a radical experiment in industrial democracy. As a recent PEP publication put it 'Proposals for worker participation in management rest upon the proposition that it is the worker's right, or upon the view that it enhances the efficiency of business.' (Shenfield, 1970) The British Steel Corporation's experiment may have been initiated for both those reasons but in comparison with the experiments which have been attempted elsewhere it cannot be seen as much more than a token gesture towards the first of these objectives.

Even such mild experiments as British Steel's should have some function in increasing the quality of boardroom decisions. Firstly, the new directors will add to the range of experience of board members. They should, secondly, reduce conflict on certain subjects if workers' directors who are sympathetic to the problems of their shop-floor colleagues can make positive contributions to policy making at an early stage. This will prevent the unions seeing policies for the first time in a potential conflict situation.

However, as far as employee rights are concerned, it is doubtful whether British Steel's workers' directors have more than a marginal effect on the prevailing situation. Nevertheless, as the Gallup figures we have quoted indicate, the existence of even a few employee directors can be of considerable symbolic significance to the workforce to the extent that employee demands for greater participation are legitimized. Experiments with workers' directors on their own do not go much beyond this symbolic significance for, as Barbara Shenfield suggests, actual employee rights are better dealt with at a lower level. As we have indicated, the chief weaknesses in the various initiatives in boardroom participation have been that they have failed to make provisions at lower levels. There was little or no attempt to build a foundation on which the top level of representation on the board could comfortably rest. This lack of participation at a lower level leaves the employee director stranded with a vast gap between his experience of decision making and the experience of his shop-floor colleagues if they have been given no role whatsoever in influencing the decisions that affect them. The importance of this factor cannot be overstated as it places the importance of employee directors firmly in context. Nor should it be thought that the mere extension of consultative rights is the answer; our own analysis of the importance of integrated systems of representation makes this clear.

The idea that employee directors merely increase the quality of boardroom decision making and have only symbolic significance for increased industrial democracy falls rather short of the greater hopes and claims which have, in the past, been inspired by the idea of workers' directors. The idea that representation on the board can make a positive contribution to industrial democracy as well as a symbolic one has been the source of considerable academic argument for years. Writers such as Clegg (1960) and Dahrendorf have found no advantages at all for the workforce in the German system, and this is the country most similar to the UK where there has been wide application of co-determination. We have in the last chapter effectively disposed of Clegg's argument that the union as a whole loses its independence when members participate in management, but the fact remains that an employee director can be faced with considerable confusion of roles.

For instance, where the German labour director is answerable to the union members of the supervisory board, his role as labour director is not defined any differently from that of an executive director in this country. Thus, although his greater knowledge of, and sympathy towards, workers' interests, ideas and needs may enable him to pay closer attention to these in decision making, his primary task is still to administer efficiently and ultimately to serve the management-designed goals of the enterprise within the constraints of the power structure and market situation in which he works.

Of course this is a simplification and it would be quite wrong to suggest that any executive director follows through his task without reference to employees' interests; but in principle his main task is to ensure the success of the enterprise. Unless this comes to be defined in a totally different way from the present definition in Western countries, there will be no possibility of a member of the executive of a firm directly representing the workers' interests. We feel therefore that to ask an employee representative to act as an executive in the conventional sense may be beneficial to both management and workforce in adding new experience to the executive team, but as soon as he is appointed he necessarily ceases to be a representative of the employees.

This effectively restricts workers' directors to the ranks of non-executive directors. In terms of the limited range of functions that we have argued is feasible within such a role, namely bringing a new perspective to bear on board deliberations and crowning and symbolizing a commitment to worker involvement in decision making, there is no reason why this should not be useful and practicable. It is true that of its nature the role of workers' director will inevitably produce tensions and conflicts between his functions as, on the one hand, a member of the board and, on the other hand, a representative of the workforce, but there is no reason why such role conflict should not be manageable and even constructive. One simple way of minimizing it is to make it explicitly clear that the workers' director sits on the board primarily as a director: his first responsibility is to the board and the over-all interests of the enterprise rather than to the workforce. Such an arrangement would quite adequately fulfil the first goal of appointing workers' directors, which is the introduction into boardroom discussions of the point of view of someone with a very different set of occupational and social experiences than is customary. This arrangement is likely to be less successful, however, with regard to the second of the two objectives, the crowning and symbolizing of commitment to worker involvement in decision making. Such a role for the workers' director is likely to ensure that he will become increasingly alienated from the workforce, and increasingly identify with the board. He will therefore increasingly lose value both as regards the contribution his different perspective can make and in putting the point of view of the workforce.

More difficult and demanding but likely to be more rewarding is the second alternative, in which the workers' director would seek to combine the roles of member of the board and representative of the workforce. For instance the BSC worker directors still spend at least half their time working on the shop floor, and efforts have been made to keep them in touch with their union colleagues through branch meetings. On the other hand, although worker directors are selected from among union nominees their appointment rests with management rather than being based on direct election by the workforce or union nomination. Moreover, while they sit on regional boards in their own areas the original concept was for them to serve on boards outside their own regions. Thus it is hardly surprising that, despite Corporation attempts to publicize the scheme, the majority of its employees are unaware of the existence of workers' director. This makes it unlikely that they would feel that their interests are represented in boardroom discussions. It is hardly surprising either that the workers' directors themselves are reported to feel no conflict of roles in these circumstances (Jones, 1971; Griffiths and Jones, 1971). Rather than a sign that the scheme is working well, however, this is more likely to indicate failure to fulfil the twin, but opposing, goals of worker representation on the board.

It seems, therefore, that even on the grounds of improving the quality of decision making, a more direct system of representation is desirable. The Donovan Commission in considering employee directors advocated a scheme whereby unions would have full powers over nominations to the board. This, however, would be likely to create a system of representation at all levels which would leave the worker feeling no greater involvement in the decisions that most affect him than he had previously.

It is interesting that the Gallup poll quoted found only 17 per cent of respondents thought that the employee directors should be appointed by the union hierarchy, while 63 per cent were in favour of direct election from the shop floor. This tends to confirm that direct election would generate more sense of involvement, although, in line with our arguments on the single channel of representation, it would be desirable for election to be organized jointly with the existing trade unions.

Our analysis, then, suggests a limited though nonetheless important role for employee directors while emphasizing the more vital need for an effective system of involvement at lower levels. It further indicates that, ideally, in order to serve their two chief functions these directors need to be explicitly employee representatives and their rights would have to be protected by their having some control over the agenda of board meetings. This would reduce the scope for the existence of caucuses outside meetings or the postponement of controversial issues in order to undermine the employee director's position. It should be noted at this point that we do not propose to support any specific form of representation. We recognize that in each company considerable differences exist. Therefore there might be a case for having a fairly homogeneous workforce represented by direct election from all the workers as one, whereas in other cases traditional rivalries would clearly have to be accommodated.

There has been no evidence of a very positive attitude on the part of UK employers to the possibility of employee directors, although entry into the EEC and the formulation of a European company law is likely to make it very much more a live issue. In the British context the BSC experiment has been brave and radical. That in a European context it seems very modest only serves to underline how slow British management has been in even starting to come to terms with the fact that the enterprise has responsibilities to groups other than its shareholders. We would accept the contention of ICI (in their recent negotiations with the signatory unions to their natural agreements) that workers' directors are not of very great importance in relation to many of the issues we have discussed. Certainly we would emphasize that a system of involvement at a lower level is much more important. Nonetheless, employers should realize that, even without the support of a system of involvement at the grass roots, employee directors may be an important symbol to the workforce. In addition to the figures we quoted above, the 1969 Gallup survey showed 56 per cent of the general public in favour of worker representation on the boards of nationalized industries. While only 47 per cent were in favour of extending this to the private sector, only 30 per cent were actually against the idea. It is fairly safe to predict that a survey of workers' feelings would elicit an even more positive response. It is in the context of such feelings that employers would be wise to initiate experiments.

Section Three

The Reform of Systems of Payment and Job Evaluation

9 Systems of payment

Many of the human and economic problems that organizations face can be traced directly to irrational, inequitable and uncontrolled systems of payment. All too often these are characterized by low base rates supplemented by a maze of plussages and premium payments for performance, attendance, special conditions, overtime, merit and shifts, whose origins are often lost in the mists of time and which are barely understood by either management or workers. The premium payments serve only to generate grievances and disputes. They accentuate wage drift by providing a discretionary component highly susceptible to bargaining pressure on supervision, whose chief goal is to get production out rather than maintain over-all wage control and differentials. They result in variations in over-all patterns of earnings between individuals and groups that owe little to real differences in either effort or job content and create for the worker insecurity and instability through a wage packet that fluctuates from week to week in a way that he can neither understand nor control.

It is hardly surprising that many of the most dramatic and prolonged strikes in recent years have been in organizations characterized by such payment systems. Stating the problem, however, is very much simpler than suggesting or, more importantly, implementing a solution. On the one hand, workers and their representatives, while seeing all the inconsistencies and inequities in the system, have also learned how to use it to their advantage: for instance, to exert pressure at critical points in production to increase rates, and to control overtime in order to increase earnings. Many managements in their turn cling to the idea that the only way to influence work behaviour is by means of direct financial incentives, and in the face of all the evidence that the situation is out of their control, maintain that they have the absolute right to determine the criteria on which wages are paid. This tendency to yield to shop-floor bargaining power while denying it any legitimacy can be seen as a basic cause of the weakening of managerial control. (Flanders, 1967)

Even if both parties wished to change, there is no perfect system of payment appropriate to all circumstances or even any particular circumstance. Merely stating the objectives that managements want their payment system to serve shows how often they are difficult to reconcile and perhaps incompatible: to reward and encourage effort while maintaining quality standards; to link the fortunes of workers with those of the enterprise and provide a framework for involvement; to attract and retain employees while at the same time maintaining an over-all distribution of earnings which corresponds to job requirements, responsibilities and effort; to encourage flexibility without creating disputes and grievances about rates and work allocation; to facilitate organizational and technological change; to give security of income while at the same time encouraging good time keeping and attendance; and to be easy to understand, administer and control.

This multiplicity underlines the two important points that management must establish the objectives it wants its payment system to serve and keep itself informed of what is happening to that payment system. All too often management lacks basic data. For instance, too rarely is there any real analysis of how hours of overtime vary from department to department, from week to week and period to period or how these are related to work load. Many of the managers we interviewed did not have this data and did not even know where to look for it.

Thus the starting points must be a policy and an information system. This chapter considers some of the factors that need to be taken into account in developing that policy into a payment system, and how far different systems of payment fulfil the different goals that we have specified. Particular attention is paid to the extent to which the payment system is consistent with the style of management that we advocated in Section Two and, indeed, we suggest that the effective reform of systems of payment can best be achieved through the application of the principles described there. Certainly there are few areas where the extension of joint regulation is more appropriate than in the case of payment systems which have got completely out of management control. The analysis will draw heavily on our own study of productivity criterion cases, about half of which involved a change in the payment system.

In terms of the actual form of a system of payment, as opposed to the principles upon which it is introduced and regulated, we must start with the theme that we have reiterated throughout the report: that the most appropriate system will depend upon the particular characteristics of a given organization. (Grinyer and Kessler, 1967)

Once again the chief sources of variation are very similar; the most immediately obvious is, perhaps, the technology of the firm concerned. Even within manufacturing industry the differences are enormous and the systems most applicable to a highly mechanized and machine-paced electronics firm and a firm in the construction industry, for instance, are likely to be entirely different. This basically comes down to the skill content and mix of jobs, their susceptibility to measurement, variations in the work flow, and the degree to which the worker can control his own work pace. A second source of variation is the nature of the labour force itself: its size, age and sex distributions, and the history of labour relations within the firm and the industry. Thirdly, the state of the market in an industry may well affect the system of payment which a firm adopts, depending on the relative emphasis put on such factors as increased production, easier recruitment, lower labour turnover and absenteeism. Fourthly come management's priorities in a given situation: for example, to maximize output, maintain quality, reduce costs, or pave the way for the acceptance of a revised payments' structure. The complexity of the interaction between these different factors can be illustrated by Lupton and Gowler's model of payment systems which identifies four groups of influences likely to affect the operation of a payment system: technology, labour markets, disputes procedures and structural characteristics. Within these categories they further identify nine measures of technology, three of labour markets, four of disputes and five of structural factors. (Lupton and Gowler, 1969)

In examining particular systems we are looking at the appropriateness of particular structures rather than attempting to evolve a method whereby the absolute level of payment is decided. In actual bargaining the latter is obviously of paramount importance to both sides, but in the day-to-day working situation, although the level of, say, basic pay is equally important to those who receive it, the problems that tend to arise spring from disagreements about the internal payment system. We are not, therefore, visualizing any major changes in the way that the wage level is decided; for, although we would hope to see those involved in bargaining fitting their decisions into a radically reconstructed framework, the bargaining itself is unlikely to change.

Individual payment by results

Of the two main types of payment system, namely time rates or payment by results, the latter, which is particularly widespread in manufacturing (42 per cent in the UK according to the ILO) but less generally used in other industries (31 per cent over-all in 1961), has aroused the greatest controversy. PBR, of course, covers a large number of very different systems but it is the disadvantages of those based on individual incentives that have become most widely recognized and there has been a move towards their replacement. This trend seems likely, though not certain, to continue; the reintroduction of an incomes policy similar to the last one might well slow down or even reverse the process. The drawbacks of individual incentives have been widely documented by both sides of industry. Such schemes tend to be irrational, difficult to understand because of the mass of complicated bonus provisions on top of a relatively low flat rate, and impossible to control. Consequently, as the NBPI reported, they certainly contribute substantially to wage drift and also seem to increase managements' as well as workers' resistance to change, possibly because of the fear that effort will immediately decrease if incentives are removed. (NBPI Report 65) Among managers and supervisors they give rise to the quite unfounded expectation that they will reduce or eliminate the need for management. Moreover such schemes rest on the assumption that workers respond to incentives purely as individuals, an assumption that is by no means fully justified by research on group behaviour or by the experience of managers trying to maximize output. Finally, from the workers' point of view they tend to create splits and tensions within the workforce, as well as lack of security in earnings.

The NBPI report did not entirely condemn individual incentive schemes, however. It set out a number of criteria by which PBR should be judged. In an optimum situation work would be measurable and directly attributable to the employee, who should himself be in control of the pace of work rather than working to a machine-set pace. There should in addition be a steady flow of work which would not be subject to frequent changes in method.

In the past the question of measurement has tended to be confined to time study but more recently has more and more been extended to the setting of work standards and the grading of jobs through evaluation. The growth of job evaluation has been prodigious in the last few years. In our own study of productivity agreements we have found job evaluation of one form or another in more than half of the agreements studied. In addition, almost all the firms with a manual workforce over a thousand had introduced job evaluation and at least half of them saw it as the most important feature of the agreement. Preliminary analysis also suggests that those deals which included job evaluation were rather more successful in the eyes of management than those without. Thus job evaluation is clearly of primary importance and, as its use is not confined to any one payment system, we shall examine it in greater detail later.

With or without job evaluation, however, individual incentive schemes will continue to have considerable drawbacks; and though they may continue to be appropriate to particular technologies, they provide a very unrewarding framework in which to develop a formal system of innvolvement. For instance, a central factor in well controlled, individual, incentive schemes is that they generally require the use of work-study techniques. Nothing prevents the decisions of work-study engineers from being the subject of negotiations, but rating consistently is a highly skilled technique which must be carried out by trained engineers and even then can be maintained only by constant checking. It is difficult to see, therefore, how the workforce can participate very greatly in work measurement and this can lead to resentment. Dalziel and Klein (1960) found that even with considerable consultation a scheme could fail through lack of understanding. For changes to gain ready acceptance, consultation must take place before rather than after they are made. We have mentioned above the one case we investigated where there had been an attempt to involve the workforce by training six men to carry out the technique themselves. This worked perfectly well but, by the time we examined the case, all six had moved permanently from the shop floor into the work-study department.

Clearly joint regulation of work measurement is possible, but only if management see the results as a basis for proposals to be negotiated in the usual way rather than as a non-negotiable set of standards. Such a procedure could not, however, be wholly satisfactory: it would be cumbersome and there would still be no guarantee that the system would be understood by the workforce and seen as rational and fair. Finally, of course, the relevance of work measurement by no means extends to all types of job and is in fact largely subject to the same conditions which the PIB set up for individual PBR schemes themselves.

Indeed far from providing a medium through which joint regulation and co-operation can be extended, individual PBR schemes tend to cause unnecessary conflict both between management and men and within management, and to create divisions within the workforce which deter it from playing a positive role in industrial relations. It is particularly noticeable in our studies, as in others, that direct workers often gain greatly at the expense of indirect workers. It would nevertheless be foolish to dismiss individual PBR out of hand if only because the extent to which it is declining is strictly limited. In our studies of productivity agreements most firms already had some system of piecework which was developed in one way or another by the agreement. While the number who moved from individual to group schemes was quite large only three firms scrapped PBR entirely while six introduced individual incentive schemes for the first time. Bean and Garside (1971) found very little evidence of a pronounced decline in PBR systems. In engineering there had been a decline from 49 to 46 per cent but, surprisingly, in the more capital intensive chemical industries, there had been a rise in the number of PBR schemes from 39 to 45 per cent. These changes took place in the period 1961–8. There will therefore continue to be many firms where individual incentive schemes are the norm because they are appropriate to that firm's work: for instance repetitive work in a plant where automation is not yet possible. Under such conditions the scheme should clearly comply as far as possible with the NBPI's criteria, with the important proviso that employees should as far as possible be involved in setting the standards for the scheme. If the principle of mutuality is formally accepted, there is greater possibility of standards no longer being thought of as something to beat, an attitude particularly frequent and damaging where individual incentives are used and where employees are working to standards about which they have been, at best, cursorily consulted. In addition, management should not leave it entirely to the stewards to communicate the nature of the deal. If communication is effective another of the recurring problems of individual incentives may be solved, the difficulty in understanding the calculations for bonuses which sometimes even management can hardly explain.

There is one further reason why we cannot simply ignore individual PBR schemes. In the past the trade unions have tended to see such schemes as iniquitous, making their members slaves to the production system, at odds with each other, and stressing output at the expense of safety and quality. Many vocal union leaders have, however, changed their view in the last few years. The AUEW has publicly proclaimed that it sees individual schemes as the best way of allowing its members to retain control over their own work, and there have been important recent examples of workers resisting the buying out of piecework because this is held to be a ruse whereby management can reassert its unilateral control over wages. What is more, it is perfectly clear that many managerial advocates of measured daywork have tended to emphasize reassertion of management control rather than joint control as the main aim of such changes in the payment system. (North and Buckingham, 1970)

However, such a development is not an inevitable consequence of moving away from individual incentives towards, for instance, a system based on measured day work, as long as the new system is based on joint regulation.

It is unfortunate that suspicion of management motives in these matters is very widespread, but this in no way means that opposition to the reform of PBR schemes is universal among trade unionists. Indeed the Government Social Survey report on Workplace Relations in 1968 showed that among shop stewards who stand to be most affected by the changes, there was a small majority (55 per cent) of those whose members worked incentive schemes who would have preferred another system. This was mainly because they wanted more security of earnings or because they disliked the inequalities in pay which tended to split their members. Moreover previous research (Hickson 1963) had shown that many workers are more interested in stability and security than in the opportunity to earn higher wages intermittently. On the other hand, it would be foolish to deny that a more formalized system of payment may reduce the area of discretion on the shop floor, at least along some dimensions. In the cases that we looked at involving a more formally regulated payment system, the trade union representatives complained in a number of instances of an increased rigidity – in, for instance, reducing the worker's discretion on how much he produced – an equal number found that their agreement had brought a reduction of close and often irksome supervision by first-line managers. There is clearly considerable opportunity for innovations that would remove some of the fears of trade unionists. It is, of course, difficult to tell what priority workers, shop stewards and full-time officials attach, in evaluating new proposals, to such factors as control over everyday working practice.

One full-time T & GWU official we interviewed expressed a strong preference for individual incentive schemes because of the control it gave his members. But the agreement which we were discussing, concluded in a large Midland engineering firm, had involved a substantial move away from individual incentives. This the official was prepared to accept because he judged that the workforce was not sufficiently well organized to resist the changes and because he trusted the management as a result of the long history of paternalism in the firm. He would not have advocated such a scheme elsewhere. This illustrates how the nature of the workforce and state of labour relations feature in trade unionists' judgements on an appropriate payment system just as it should in managements. What is clear, and emphasized by the figures in the Social Survey report, is that there exists considerable scope as well as need for change, and it would be unfortunate if this opportunity was dissipated because of management's failure to recognize its existence, and will the means.

Group incentive schemes

Some of what we have been saying applies as much to group incentive schemes as to individual ones; in these we do not include plant-wide schemes but simply the paying of bonuses on the performances of a workgroup rather than an individual. The most immediately attractive features of such schemes are the flexibility which they permit and the co-operation they encourage within the workgroup. The group performance on which the bonus is based may be that of a maintenance team of three men or a department of fifty. The main disadvantage is probably the fact that such a scheme retains some of the divisive features of the individual scheme in terms of both fragmented bargaining and divided workforce and may be equally prone to the development of anomalies and inequities between groups and 'leap-frogging' in wage claims. For instance, before moving into measured day work, Vauxhalls found that their group bonus had become so taken for granted that it completely lost its incentive purpose. The scheme also began to militate against co-operation and change in the same way as many individual incentives do. (King, 1964) Nonetheless such a system may be quite appropriate in a plant where departments have very distinct functions and little contact with each other.

The most successful example of a group incentive scheme that we encountered involved a large modern warehouse employing about one hundred men. The technology was such that the men split up naturally into teams, each in the charge of a supervisor, whose salary depended on the output of his team. The results of the scheme allowed the firm to adopt a five-day week, instead of seven, to substantially improve recruitment and decrease absenteeism and labour turnover. The firm had tried an individual scheme initially but quickly changed to the group scheme, which worked well. It was successful primarily because bonuses were linked to natural work groups, membership of which had meaning for workers and where results could be directly linked to the efforts of the work group. Where there are no 'natural' groups whose performance can be measured, there seems no justification for trying to impose group schemes; in such cases a plant-wide scheme might be more appropriate. Assuming, however, the existence of departments with clearly defined sections, group schemes may well have considerable advantages, particularly in terms of employee involvement, as they create natural units for discussion, consultation and decision making. On the other hand, it is interesting to note that the management of the warehouse mentioned above, when asked about future plans, notwithstanding the success of their existing group incentive system, by-passed the idea of a plant-wide PBR scheme and said they were examining the possibilities of measured day work.

This highlights a further feature of our findings. In many cases management had substantially raised output and productivity by introducing group or departmental bonus schemes; but there were signs that these short-term benefits were achieved at the expense of longer-term costs; as anomalies developed in the relative earnings of different groups, as the market situation changed or as the need arose for changes in production methods. The way in which group incentives can bring about striking, short-term benefits while generating longer-term problems suggests that the reform of a payment system can be seen as a two-phase process. Where an enterprise is suffering from both low productivity and an irrational system of payment it might be well advised to introduce a group incentive scheme initially to raise the level of productivity and tempo of work, and then move on to measured day work or a plant-wide bonus system.

Plant-wide bonus schemes

The plant-wide bonus scheme sets out to achieve some of the benefits of the group incentive scheme while avoiding anomalies and inequities between different groups. They are distinct in principle from the individual or small group schemes in that their main objective is normally not to provide a direct financial incentive but to encourage employees to feel involved in the performance of the team and interested in its affairs. (Bolle de Bal 1970) An across-the-board bonus is paid to all employees depending − sometimes very loosely indeed − on their collective performance. The best known of these schemes are the Scanlon and Rucker plans, although it has been suggested that most plant bonus schemes relate far less specifically to output than do genuine Scanlon and Rucker plans. (Corina, 1967) The Scanlon is more explicitly concerned with participation and is calculated on the basis of the sales value of production while 'added value' is the basis for calculation in the Rucker plan.

In our studies we came across only one scheme which management éxplicity described as a Scanlon plan, but there were some that approximated to the concept.

Perhaps the most important feature of such schemes is that, as conceived by Scanlon, they must be based on close communication and consultation between manager and managed. And in the case we studied, where the plant was mostly engaged in process technology, there was indeed much greater consultation than there had ever been before and both management and unions were enthusiastic about the state of labour relations as a result of the deal. Management felt it had been very worthwhile in its immediate financial effects. The bonus was calculated by guaranteeing that if the wage and salary bill for the workforce came to less than one per cent of the production value, the difference would be shared out. Problems arose, however, because in the first two months the older of the two plants did not achieve any bonus owing to adverse market conditions. Subsequently there were substantial redundancies in that plant although the company had been running it down anyway and claimed this was not connected with the new scheme. As a result the company set up a reserve pool in order to stablize bonus earnings for the workforce and in bad months it supplemented the pool. Nonetheless after the first two-year agreement another was signed for three years with little opposition.

The experience of this company ties in very closely with the opinions expressed by the NBPI in Report No. 65 which concluded that such schemes needed a 'generally favourable market situation and are seen as susceptible as any other schemes to "wearing out".' The managing director in our case admitted that it was difficult to keep steam up and that the scheme could be a source of dissatisfaction when the firm was doing badly. Another case we looked at involved a scheme whereby all the former bonuses men had earned were consolidated and a uniform bonus, based on production, was introduced on top. This was reviewed quarterly and kept stable by a reserve fund. Once again managerial objectives (lower turnover, easier recruitment) were very largely achieved, but because the firm hit a bad patch economic targets were not achieved. In this situation the stable bonus was shown to be a danger as the workforce very quickly came to expect it as of right, and good industrial relations were retained only by maintaining it. Both these cases lead us to accept the conclusion of the NBPI that Scanlon/ Rucker plans' main advantage is that they involve a thorough rethink of the relationship between employer and employee.

Moreover it is quite clear that since most plant bonus schemes are primarily concerned with social rather than directly financial objectives, it is less likely that strict economic control will be maintained; most deals therefore seem liable to move away from Scanlon and Rucker's original conceptions of how they should work. This does not, however, mean that firms cannot become more efficient with plant bonus schemes; in many ways they can and have. As far as the social objectives are concerned consultation and participation are almost necessarily increased because of the difficulty of introducing such schemes without them. Nonetheless, as Bolle de Bal points out, plant bonus schemes are often introduced by management to reassert control, with participation as a mere corollary. There is nothing wrong in wanting to get rid of an uncontrollable incentive scheme but we feel that plant bonus schemes of the type we have described can be no more than a temporary expedient without the active participation of the workforce in regulating them. They offer a possible framework for encouraging greater involvement but by no means the only one.

Profit sharing

There remains the other plant- or company-based scheme which seeks to link employees' remuneration even more explicitly to the performance and well-being of the firm. This is, of course, profit sharing where the bonus is related directly to the dividends paid to shareholders. In principle, this type of scheme would seem to have many advantages in that it gives employees a degree of ownership of the business as well as a share in its success. The idea of profit sharing has, therefore, enjoyed some popularity amongst trade unionists and an element of progressive management. Thus, in a large engineering firm we studied, the stewards were very keen to replace worn-out sectional productivity agreements with a profit-sharing scheme.

Management baulked at the idea on the grounds that the workforce should only get rewards from its direct contribution. But whatever the argument for and against profit sharing in principle we cannot see it playing any more than a very marginal part in bringing about any greater feelings of involvement in the job and the enterprise. As Lupton points out, workers may find their bonus very welcome and may even decide to stay on with the firm because of it; but they will find difficulty in relating their efforts to the bonus they receive (more important if the profit-sharing scheme is the whole payment system rather than just an additional payment), they will have little direct control over it and little sympathy with it. (Lupton, 1969) We would accept these conclusions but add that it seems unlikely that the bonus will be welcomed on the basis of its relationship with the profits. At the time of negotiation the profit-sharing idea might be very popular; but when the bonus is due to be paid out it may be viewed in a strictly instrumental fashion and there would therefore be no more sympathy for management's position or acceptance of it if the profits – and therefore the bonus – fell than in any other similar situation.

Lupton's remarks point directly to the distinction which we have been at pains to draw throughout, that of satisfaction with a job and satisfaction in a job. Profit sharing may well increase satisfaction with a job as long as there are substantial profits and may therefore induce a worker to take the job, or, as Lupton says, to stay in it. Such a scheme is unlikely, however, to increase involvement in the job, which is our main concern here. We conclude therefore that, in favourable market circumstances, profit sharing may be a useful addition to the primary system of payment but not an alternative to it for it would in effect become a negative incentive. Even in favourable circumstances, as a supplement to the primary system, its chief effect will be more to contribute to a climate in which greater co-operation is possible – given the managerial will – rather than directly bringing about increased co-operation.

Measured day work

Perhaps the most important development in payment systems has been the growing popularity of measured day work, at least amongst management. It is in the case of MDW that job evaluation comes most strongly into its own. MDW is set up by careful grading of jobs, after which the worker is paid a stable wage for a measured work load according to his grade. Once grade, work load and wage have been established, they will change only as a result of changes in the job structure and general increases in earnings. It would seem, therefore, on the face of it that workers lose some of the day-to-day control over their earnings and pace and volume of work that they enjoyed under individual incentive schemes.

The decline in this type of fragmented, informal control may be compensated by an increase in stability and security of earnings, and may moreover give rise to a different and more constructive type of control through joint regulation. Many of the employers who have pioneered the introduction of MDW have tended to be among the more progressive, and they have sought the involvement and agreement of workers and their representatives in the implementation of the change. Indeed such radical changes would normally be impossible if they were not agreed and their implementation and operation monitored and supervised on a joint basis. In this way day-to-day control on the shop floor gives way to joint control at a higher level. It is clear that these different types of control may have varying degrees of appeal for different types of worker and shop steward, and certainly some stewards have fought MDW bitterly because they saw it eroding their influence on the shop floor. But, in line with our general argument in Section Two, we see formalized joint control and regulation as the most effective means of combining worker involvement in decision making with efficient working.

Thus, not only are the opportunities for employee involvement in decision making as great, though of a different order, within MDW as under individual incentive schemes, but they are just as great as under plant-wide incentive schemes. MDW may not provide the same framework for and impetus to the inauguration of co-operation and a consultative style of management, but in so far as it requires agreement and joint decision making on the nature of tasks, grading and pay initially, and the continuing joint monitoring of these, then it offers a framework for a different kind of constructive involvement in aspects of the job that are of basic importance. The way in which differentials are controlled within MDW, the way earnings are less affected by factors outside the workers' control, together with the fact that the system is more easily understandable than PBR, should lead it to be regarded as a more equitable system of payment. Indeed the implication within the type of application of MDW that we have described, that the employee does not have standards imposed from above but agrees to them, is 'as clear a recognition as anything in a Scanlon/Rucker-type plan that unilateral management decision making in areas of direct importance to the employee is neither constructive nor, increasingly, feasible. Apart from shop-floor and shop-steward resistance to the introduction of new systems devised by management alone, the official policy of trade unions is increasingly requiring acceptance of the principle of mutuality as a precondition of negotiation on new systems of pay.

One of the chief preoccupations of management with regard to the introduction of MDW is that the removal of direct financial incentives will result in a reduction in effort. The NBPI report concluded that this did sometimes occur, although the Board suggested that the effect was merely a temporary one. It was, however, unable to establish certain likely effects of MDW on the relationships between performance and cost. The few instances which we came across in our research suggest a somewhat mixed picture. In one case, a Lancashire engineering firm, a traditional piecework system was replaced by time rates. For the next three years output dropped slowly until it was felt necessary to reintroduce financial incentives, this time on a group basis.

A second case, a mechanical-engineering plant in South Wales, was less clearcut. The introduction of MDW had not given the yields achieved under the former PBR system but had got the firm away from the inbuilt escalating conflicts of the old system. Interestingly the union had put considerable pressure on management to abandon piecework. In the third situation there were no complaints about decreasing production. The workforce was placed in bands according to performance, which was evaluated every three months by a committee on which the unions had 50 per cent representation. The only problem was that there was some drift, and the firm found that the workers in the south-east plant tended to be concentrated in the top bands while the Scottish employees were largely in the bottom two bands.

It is clear that we cannot draw any meaningful conclusions from these few examples. In the cases studied by the NBPI the companies seemed generally to achieve considerable economic benefits from the changes. Chief among these were a more stable and secure basis for forecasting costs, fewer interruptions to work and the creation of a better climate in which to introduce change. But if the removal of direct financial incentives is not to result in any decline in effort, it requires that management, and particularly first-line management, accept the task of managing that it formerly and mistakenly left to the payment system. Management has to ensure a steady flow of work and make available the tools and materials to do the job, rather than wait for workers to ask for them so that they can maintain their earnings. And management must pay a great deal more attention to non-financial incentives: to social relationships, styles of supervision, job content and enrichment. Certainly in the case that we looked at where management concluded that the removal of direct financial incentives had resulted in a decline in production, it could equally have been argued that bad management had brought about this decline. In other words we should not expect any uniform result from a change to MDW. On the one hand, some firms have felt the lack of incentives; but on the other hand there has been much research to show that over 50 per cent of pieceworkers do not understand how their wage is calculated – hardly likely to make for very effective incentives. (Shimmin, 1959; Marriott, 1961)

Beyond this, one variation of MDW which permits the reintroduction of a degree of financial incentive as well as some opportunity for advancement among workers is the Premium Payments Plan as introduced, for instance, by Philips Industries Ltd. This is a form of MDW within which there is a graded system based on job evaluation, but within each grade workers are rated and paid a differential according to performance and merit and have the incentive of moving up to a higher level within the grade if they are able. (Westwood, 1965) This system depends very heavily on a realistic and consistent basis for measurement acceptable both to employer and employee. As devised by Philips, whose PPP is best known, the level at which the worker is paid is worked out between him and his supervisor, on whom incidentally the responsibility for the successful administration of the scheme largely lies. Philips found the plan very satisfactory, particularly in improving and stabilizing labour relations. It is, however, difficult to draw hard conclusions on the Philips plan because of the lack of disinterested research on it. The research done and published has largely been undertaken by Philips management. (Mopham, 1964; Parsons, 1966)

It seems, however, that such a scheme would be very difficult to introduce into the types of organization where the reform of decayed piece work or individual incentive schemes is most needed. Workers in such situations would be very unlikely to accept a merit or performance-rating system that was unilaterally devised and operated by management, for exactly the same reasons as the workers in our case study in Section Two were reluctant to let management decide upon promotion unilaterally. The applications of PPP which the NBPI looked at mainly involved women workers and women have always been very much more willing to accept unilateral, management decision making than men. For instance, it has frequently been noted under individual incentive schemes how women tend to accept rates unquestioningly while men tend to regard them as negotiable and seek to change them.

This does not mean that PPP is intrinsically incompatible with joint regulation and would be impossible to introduce in heavily unionized situations where unilateral management decision making is strongly resisted. It seems quite feasible in such situations that after

MDW had been successfully introduced and the improvements in the climate of industrial relations experienced, a **PPP** system could be developed on a joint basis. The criteria for rating merit and performance would have to be devised jointly, accepted by the workers as equitable, and criteria which are seen as pandering to 'blue-eyed boys' and 'company men' such as 'loyalty' and 'co-operativeness' would have to be avoided. If introduced on this basis such a scheme would have the benefit for management of encouraging effort and performance within a controlled system while being consistent with workers' seemingly incompatible ideas that good performance should be rewarded but that the reward system should not divide and fragment the workforce. Moreover the system is able to accommodate very real difference in capacity and ability depending upon age and experience. Again the system is quite consistent with increases in earnings – through increases in the rate for the grade – on the bases of comparability, profitability, rises in the cost of living, and increases within the system through promotion up the grades and merit within the grades.

We draw our conclusions to this chapter after some consideration of job evaluation in the next.

10 Job evaluation

A common characteristic of virtually all reforms of payment systems is that they are based on systematic job evaluation. It is a truism that there are no pay disputes, only disputes about differentials: disputes about an individual's or group's pay in relation to other individuals or groups. In terms of minimizing grievances, and overt and unconstructive conflict, there is no more vital a change needed than the development of systems for analysing the content of jobs and attaching a value to them relative to other jobs. This must be founded on the highest degree of consensus within the organization about the bases on which employees should be rewarded differentially. Remuneration must then be geared to those evaluations. In a sense this is what management has always done, in so far as it has paid different rates for different jobs; but it has not done so systematically. It has tended to do so arbitrarily and unilaterally in a way that has not kept pace with technological change, growth in the size of the organization and the decay in systems of payment. Thus there has been a tendency for differentials in jobs to reflect traditional and historical distinctions that bear little relationship to the current content of the job, as well as variations between the bargaining strengths of different groups, and the scope their pay system provides for drift.

Essentially job evaluation should seek to do systematically, rationally and jointly what management has attempted in the past to do unthinkingly, arbitrarily and unilaterally. This does not mean that there is any system of job evaluation which provides an objective, absolute measure of the value of jobs, independently of the differing values of management and different groups of employees. Indeed, within job evaluation, it is important to distinguish between two distinct, but often confused, aspects. The first of these is a set of analytical tools that now enable us to describe with some exactness the content of jobs: the degree of skill, knowledge, qualification, experience, mental ability, manual dexterity, that the work requires; the responsibility carried; the degree of stress and discomfort involved; the amount of physical effort required; and so on. The development of techniques for job description now means that this can result in an objective analysis of the job. But in addition to this the process of evaluation involves a second, more subjective, stage. This consists of attaching a weight or value to the objective characteristics of the jobs and a mechanism whereby these values can be translated into the money rate for the job. Thus while it is possible to describe objectively the level of education required to do a job, the weight that should be attached to differences in educational requirements in the evaluation of the job is essentially a matter of social values. And while it is clear that within our society there is a relatively wide consensus and shared set of values, however implicit, about the relative value that should be placed on different job requirements, there is also room for genuine disagreement. Thus the value placed upon educational qualifications may reasonably be assumed to relate to one's own level of education, the value placed on physical effort to the effort involved in one's job, and the value on stress to the stress in one's job. In this way it is necessary for an effective system of job evaluation to involve both an objective measurement of jobs and a mechanism whereby the highest degree of consensus about the value of different job dimensions can be built into the ratings of jobs for the purpose of remuneration. Job evaluation then is the systematic application of a set of values about different job dimensions, backed up by certain analytical tools.

This preamble is necessary because there is a tendency for management to promote, and even to believe, the idea that in job evaluation it has an authoritative independent tool for determining job grades and differentials, legitimized by science; and that anyone who questions the form and findings of a job evaluation system is either a fool or a knave. However we regard the subjective element in job evaluation not as a weakness but a strength, in so far as it requires a high degree of worker involvement in the formulation and introduction of effective and equitable job evaluation systems. Moreover not only is such involvement necessary for the success of schemes, and all the indications suggest that success is directly related to the degree of worker involvement, but also this involvement represents a further channel for the development of just the t; pe of constructive relationship between management and labour that we have been advocating throughout our report. Thus the search for a job evaluation system that is wholly objective and universally applicable is not only unrealistic, but also intrinsically undesirable. The longer-term benefits of introducing job evaluation as a means for improving industrial relations and as a channel of worker involvement, as well as a basis for equitable pay, depend on the system being worked out, designed and implemented jointly by management and men in a particular context; job evaluation is not an inviolate system imposed from above and sanctioned by reference to external authority.

Different systems of job evaluation

In its report on job evaluation the NBPI found that about a quarter of all workers were covered by some form of job evaluation system, and the Board expected this to rise to something over a third within a few years. (NBPI report, 1968) It looked at the four chief forms of job evaluation in use: ranking, grading, factor comparison and points-assessment systems. Each of these basic systems has differing intrinsic strengths and weaknesses, making it more or less appropriate to different situations depending essentially upon size and the number of different jobs in a plant.

Ranking is very simple as it ranks jobs over-all, normally through job description, rather than dividing them up into various components. The most and least important jobs are identified and two or three ranks are established in between. Jobs are then grouped round the 'key jobs' at either end of the scale with subsidiary groups in between. The main drawback is that it is not possible by this method to establish the real level of difference between jobs, particularly in a large enterprise.

Grading starts at the opposite end from ranking. Whereas the latter divides the jobs into grades after ranking them, grading sets out the number and characteristics of the grades and then carries out the job description process. When this is done the various jobs are fitted into the existing grades. Like ranking this method does not break jobs up into their component parts and therefore does not readily apply to a complex situation where there is either a large number of very different jobs, or where the jobs are difficult to define as a whole.

Factor comparison, on the other hand, splits jobs up into either four or five different factors. For manual workers, these are: physical, mental and skill content, environment and amount of responsibility. A number of 'key jobs' are identified, split into factors and a rank is produced on the basis of relative importance of each factor. The individual factors are then described in relation to the amount of the wage which they justify. It is at this point that the major difficulty is encountered, for it is extremely difficult to make the relationship between a particular factor and a percentage of the subject's wage easily understandable to the subject.

The points' system has been by far the most widely used in this country. It involves the analysis of a number of job factors which will differ in kind and in number according to the jobs being evaluated. These factors are carefully defined and each one has a range of points allocated to it, with the maximum depending on its significance in relation to other factors. Once again a number of key jobs are described and evaluated initially. This is then done for all the jobs and each factor in a job is compared with the originally defined factor and a number of points awarded. A ranking order is established by the sum of all the points which a job has been awarded. These are fitted into a number of established grades and then translated into money.

The chief attraction of this mode has generally been that it can cover the widest range of possible factors and, more important, it puts all the subjective elements in job evaluation into a predetermined structure. This has been welcomed in the past because job evaluation was seen not just simply as a means of providing an objective framework within which values could be best expressed, but also as part of the attempt to develop an entirely objective, and therefore universally acceptable wage structure. Although the NBPI expressed this desire for greater objectivity, the report on job evaluation had to admit the dangers which the points' system, in fact, highlights.

First the method assumes that the factors used will be adequate to describe all jobs. It also assumes an arbitrary numerical unit, namely the point. Thirdly, it assumes the inbuilt weightings are constant and widely applicable. Fourthly, consistency is particularly difficult to maintain in a large organization when many assessors are used; and, finally, one point can make a great deal of difference, which can be seen as inequitable. In other words, the system is inclined to rigidity and pretends to a degree of objectivity which in its basic form it does not have.

In addition to these basic methods, there are some single-factor systems such as Jacques's 'Time span of discretion'. (Jacques, 1961) In so far as this has not been found to be widely usable among manual workers, or certainly has not been successfully applied to a union-organized labour force, it might not seem to warrant a great deal of consideration. But it is interesting because it represents just the type of approach to job evaluation that we have suggested was unconstructive in industrial relations terms. Essentially Jacques claims to have discovered, through research, the key variable which determines the subjective evaluation of the worth of different jobs among all types of workers from the managing director to unskilled labourers. And this key variable, he concludes, is level of responsibility as measured by the worker's 'time-span of discretion', that is to say 'the maximum period of time during which the use of discretion is authorized and expected without review of that discretion by a superior.' The longer the worker can go without having his performance checked, the greater the responsibility he carries and the greater the worth of his job on both his own and other people's valuation. Thus the time span of discretion involved in all jobs should be measured, renumeration geared to the degree of discretion and all will be satisfied because their renumeration is determined by what is universally the source of subjective ratings of the relative worth of different jobs.

Leaving aside the question of the extent to which Jacques's research demonstrates that basically there is just this one shared criterion of fairness (and this hardly corresponds with the experience of those seeking to implement job evaluation schemes), it is worth looking at what the application of his method would involve in practice. It would involve a group of workers and their representatives accepting, first, that this external authority, science (and indeed that most questionable of all sciences, psycho-analysis), had established that there was just this one criterion for determining equitable payment, and there was no questioning this because it was scientific. It would involve them in accepting that the ratings would have to be carried out by a skilled technician, because the measurement is such an expert task that it requires long training based on high intelligence, and that there would be no questioning the ratings because they were objective. So, as well question the length of a piece of string, and that a longer piece of string should cost more than a shorter one, as question the differentials produced by the application of equitable payment through the time span of discretion.

Thus the workers and their representatives have to accept the system without involvement and without understanding. There is here no scope for the use of job evaluation as a constructive medium for joint decision making. In so far as we have argued that, all other things being equal, greater involvement and greater understanding are desirable in their own right and for the creation of healthy industrial relations, it would have to be demonstrated that this system produced strikingly better results than other job-evaluation systems requiring involvement and understanding on the part of the work force for it to be preferred to them. This demonstration we do not have. Jacques of course would claim that the end would justify the means, as the end result would be a pattern of differentials that corresponded most closely to felt fair pay. All we can say on this is that workers' conscious ideas do not square with this proposition, however much he and his colleagues may have detected it in their subconscious or unconscious feelings. Moreover we are unlikely to be able to put the pudding to the test of eating. Where the system has been applied it has largely been among professional, managerial and clerical workers, where we would accept that level of responsibility is more generally accepted as a chief criterion for differentials, or among non-unionized manual workers. In situations where unilateral management decision making is not accepted so unquestioningly – and we have argued such situations are many and growing – management is not going to get very far by trying to introduce such a system. (Fox, 1966) What is required in these circumstances is something that the workforce can fully understand, can become involved in, and, through their representatives, can influence and agree. However we do not discount the value of the concept of time span of discretion as a tool for organizational analysis, only question the claims made for it as a universally applicable tool for solving the problem of pay differentials.

More sophisticated variations of conventional methods are now being developed that promise to be more productive on those criteria. Two examples are the Urwick Orr Profile Method and the AIC Direct Consensus System, both of which require a high degree of worker involvement.

The profile method takes a number of jobs and evaluates them using unweighted factors. This process is carried out by a joint committee. The same jobs are then subjected to paired comparison to obtain a ranking value. The two tables can then be related to obtain factor weights. This method takes into account the fact that the aptitudes a man brings to work will be used at a certain level depending on various technological and managerial factors. Job characteristics or factor weights can therefore be chosen only after the range of work involved is identified. The characteristics must reflect both the range of the work and those aspects of the job which the employee sees as important. These two needs are satisfied by the dual approach described above. The important feature is that weighting depends on the employees' own evaluation. They must therefore be involved from the start if a mutually acceptable rate is to be devised.

AIC's direct consensus method is based on perhaps an even higher degree of worker involvement. After choosing a sample of jobs, a straightforward job description is carried out by the subject himself. The task thereafter is to rank jobs and the drawbacks of the simple ranking method can be completely eliminated because with the application of electronic data processing each job can be compared with every other job. (AIC, 1968) When the paired comparison process is completed, a dozen or so members of the various interest groups involved assess a number of pairs on the basis of a general definition, such as job worth. The jobs are assessed as a whole and, on the basis of the number of times each job has been preferred, a rank order is drawn up. The effect of eccentric decisions is minimized by taking account of the calibre of jobs to which any individual job is preferred. The central feature of this method is that it recognizes the subjective nature of job evaluation and makes use of it. In a recent agreement in a Midlands industrial truck plant, for instance, the shop floor had majority representation on the grading committee and their subjective decisions were computed to create an entirely acceptable wage structure.

A third approach worth mentioning briefly is that adopted by ICI in the application of its weekly staff agreement. Here management and workers worked out job descriptions jointly and then presented them to visiting panels made up of management representatives, none of whom was associated with the particular works. There was a very high degree of worker involvement in the development of the job analyses and descriptions within shop-floor discussion groups, joint working parties and joint co-ordinating committees. One of the chief purposes of these exercises was to examine how jobs could be reorganized and restructured in order to inject into them maximum amount of interest, meaning and scope for the use of abilities, thus not only bringing about a degree of job enrichment, but also qualifying workers for the highest possible rating under the evaluation system. The chief strength of this approach was the very high level of involvement in the analyses and reorganization, together with the fact that, in front of the visiting panel, local plant management and workers were seen as batting on the same side. Local management were as concerned about building up jobs as high as possible, about impressing the panel with how rich different jobs were and achieving as high a rating for the jobs as were the workers, once the descriptions had been thrashed out jointly at local level. However, the success of the scheme was dependent upon the grading panel being seen as independent and expert, rather than its judgements being legitimized by worker involvement, for no worker representative or trade unionist sat on the panel.

This approach also illustrates the way in which job evaluation can and should be used as a tool of organizational analysis and change. In our discussion of it we have focused very much on its importance as a technique for helping with the process of establishing wage differentials. But this represents only part of its potential. Its application should involve not merely analysing and describing existing jobs within the existing organization as a basis for evaluating these. It should involve a more creative stage. That is, after describing the existing situation, there should be a process of critically examining the present job mix and job contents with a view to seeing how tasks, functions and responsibilities could be re-allocated to bring about more efficient working and more meaningful jobs. This was the feature of the ICI application that was quite as important as the devising of a simpler and more rational system of payment – if not more so.

Thus we see the development and extension of systematic job evaluation as crucial to efficient operation, to job enrichment and to equitable payment. It is also a medium for bringing about a greater degree of worker involvement and joint regulation of the criteria on which employees are remunerated. Trade unionists have sometimes been suspicious of the application of job evaluation, and this is justified where the management approach has been one based on the idea that it has a magic formula which will resolve all conflicts about relative earnings and the criteria for differentials, that this must be accepted because it is objective and legitimized by science so that anything worker and work groups have to say about it must be irrational and special pleading. Where the approach that we have advocated is adopted, however, we suggest that systematic job evaluation is as much in the worker's and trade unionist's interests as in the management's. It represents one more example of a move away from management, on the one side, claiming the right of unilateral, arbitrary decision making, and the unions, on the other, in practice exercising control through permitting no change and defending irrational inefficient practices from fear of unrestrained management discretion and prerogatives. And it represents a move towards greater joint control and constructive change through involvement.

In order to be effective on all these counts, however, job evaluation needs to be a continuous process rather than being seen as a 'one-off' exercise. It is not simply a matter of setting up a joint committee to oversee the introduction of a new system of rational evaluation and grading which, once established, will last for ever. Immediately after the introduction of the new system there will be a number of objections to the results, which will have to be jointly reviewed and judged. Thereafter jobs will change, new plant will be introduced, individuals and work groups will exert pressure to get themselves graded more highly, thus creating the danger of drift and growing anomalies. All this requires that there be permanent institutions in being for the assessment and re-evaluation of jobs to maintain equity and prevent the development of a further source of wage drift.

Conclusions on the reform of systems of payment and job evaluation

One of the most striking things about the effects of the attempts to reform payment systems in different ways that we have looked at, in both our own research and other people's, is the similarity of the claims made for them by the managements and unions involved.

Thus whether they have introduced a group incentive scheme, a plant-wide incentive scheme, measured day work, or a conventional productivity agreement, they all tended to feel that the change had been very worthwhile for much the same reasons. And essentially these were that the process of change, the process of joint consultation and joint decision making that brought about the change, had also brought about a healthier, more constructive set of relationships between management, unions and workers. This suggests that the process of change and the way that change is brought about is, on some criteria, more important than the content or form of the change itself. It suggests that what was important was less that a Scanlon plan, measured day work or a group incentive scheme was being introduced, than that management and unions were getting together within new institutions on a joint basis, to work out a new system together. Communications improved, information was shared, relationships were changed because attention was being focused on an area which was of key importance to all parties, and this attention was leading to action. It is for this reason that we are disinclined to call for improved communications, increased joint consultation, and a greater sharing of information in general and abstract terms. The theme that has been running through our report is the need for the extension of joint regulation and joint decision making that require such improvements if they are to be successful.

There are, of course, other reasons why in many of these cases, whatever the form and content of the change, it was welcome for much the same reasons. First, the firms had often been going through a very bad patch both in industrial relations and economic terms before the change, and often these were so bad that any change could only have been for the better. Secondly, given the myriad, inbuilt damaging effects of decayed piece work or individual incentive schemes, any move away from these in such circumstances to a more collective approach, whether the unit was the group or the plant, could similarly only be for the better. Associated with this is the evidence we have quoted that there is among both workers and shop stewards a widespread attitude favourably disposed to a move away from individual incentives.

Thus, while we conclude that the process, the method, and even the simple fact of change, are often more important than the form or content of the change itself, and while we repeat that different systems of payment will be more or less appropriate to different circumstances, we see and welcome a general trend away from systems based on individual incentives. The need and tendency for this to happen has been brought about by a number of changes in industry.

These include, first, the increase in the size of plants and the interdependence of plants which place a premium upon systems of payment that encourage harmonious relationships, and minimize the possibility of interruptions to work, rather than those that seek to maximize effort at the risk of generating disputes and grievances. Secondly, technological change is modifying the content of jobs in a way that means that they demand less expenditure of effort and more vigilance, responsibility and conscientiousness. While this is happening and has happened more quickly within industries based on advanced technology, like oil and chemicals, it is also likely to be the trend in other industries. Thirdly, management's acceptance of greater involvement by workers in company affairs may often be incompatible with individual incentives which may tend to encourage non-involvement. (Klein, 1964)

What this trend also means, as we have emphasized, is that the move away from individual incentives highlights the need for improved management, particularly, first, in regulating the flow of work and ensuring the availability of tools and materials; and secondly, in paying increasing attention to non-financial motivation as described in Sections One and Two.

As to which variations of different systems of payment firms move on to, we have briefly described the strengths and weaknesses of the broad categories available, and suggest that choice should be related to a detailed analysis of individual priorities and circumstances. It is clear for instance that any scheme which has as its primary objective the desire to provide a financial incentive is going to be liable, to some degree to the sorts of weaknesses that have been all too apparent in our analysis. We have even suggested that the process of change may sometimes be usefully seen as a series of phased developments and refinements. Thus a firm with low productivity and a decayed piecework system might reasonably see itself changing to a group or plant bonus scheme, then on to a basic MDW system and subsequently on to a Premium Payment Plan over a period of ten years.

The way in which different systems are appropriate to different situations at different points in time can well be illustrated by the relationship between system of pay and involvement. It is clear that there is no system of payment or refinement on a basic system that automatically brings about a high degree of co-operation, participation and involvement. The important change needed to bring this about is for management increasingly to create and encourage the development of mechanisms, channels and institutions for involvement that relate to action, and the aspects of work that are important to workers. But it may be that a particular kind of reward system can facilitate this type of development and help to get it started, although again, the form that this takes may need to vary with the nature of the labour force involved. Thus, given a compliant labour force that willingly accepts the principle of unilateral management decision making, it may be sufficient to pay 10 per cent above the going rate to provide a situation in which workers feel generously rewarded and a framework within which involvement of the participative, consultative and co-operative type can be developed. At the other end of the spectrum with a highly organized labour force, which effectively exercises control by not accepting many changes that management would like to make, the productivity-bargaining approach may be a prerequisite of effective involvement and successful change. This requires that changes be agreed within what is essentially a bargaining rather than a consultative context, and most importantly the direct financial benefits of the changes being shared on an agreed basis between the firm and the workers. In between these opposite ends of the continuum some variation on the group- or plant-bonus system may provide an appropriate economic framework within which a collaborative system can be developed, now based on consultation, now on negotiation. But in each case the reward system will be essentially a facilitator for management initiative and changes in management practice, rather than a causative factor which brings about the changes directly. Thus some mechanism for demonstrating that the results of involvement and collaboration are shared on an equitable basis is often very useful for initiating such changes and developing different attitudes and habits, but the important thing in the long term is management will and practice, and the sharing of benefits on the basis of traditional collective bargaining at set periods can equally be a sufficient framework for involvement.

The way in which we have described different formulas for distributing the benefits of change as facilitators and frameworks illustrates our general conclusion on systems of payment, which is that they are far more potent as a negative force than as a positive one. In other words if a firm has an irrational, inequitable payment system, it is likely to sour employee/employer relations regardless of any other conditions and practices. A rational, equitable, agreed system does not have a positive effect to the same degree. It creates the conditions for harmonious relationships, and indeed, it is a pre-condition to harmonious relationships, but it does not automatically bring them about. The extent to which constructive labour relations of the type we have advocated are brought about will depend upon the extent to which managers can develop new habits of management within the framework of a satisfactory system of payment.

11 General conclusions

Introduction

The present state of employee and industrial relations in the UK can bring little satisfaction to anyone, workers, trade unionists, management, shareholders or the community at large. This is not to say that we throw up our hands in horror at the number of strikes, lock-outs or sacking of employees in industrial disputes. In a free society, whose industrial relations are ultimately based on collective bargaining between employers and employee representatives, it is by definition always possible for one party to say 'this we cannot accept', which results in a strike or lock-out. That this will sometimes happen is unavoidable. Moreover as well as often being costly for both parties and damaging to industrial relations strikes can often also have beneficial results, directing management's attention to aspects of its business that it had neglected, encouraging management to come to terms with the realities of the power situation it faces and recognize and respect the need and necessity for effective employee representation, and to develop or revise institutions, procedures or systems of payment. For instance, the strike at Pilkington's brought about a massive management rethink on the system of payment, system of collective bargaining and forms of representation. And we have seen how a recognition strike generated a representative body without which management could not have introduced a major reorganization of the payment system and job evaluation.

The changes could, of course, have been brought about without a strike and the individual and corporate losses would have been less severe had there not been a strike. The lasting bitterness that may ensue from a major strike makes it a high price to pay for any benefits it brings. Consequently it would be infinitely preferable if managements paid sufficient attention to industrial relations and the aspects of their business that affect them without being forced to do so by manifest conflict. But in the real world not all managements are going to be doing all the thinking, planning and reorganization with regard to the way they manage people that they should. Often they will pay attention only to aspects of their business that demand attention and will neglect anything that, although not perfect, does not seem to create immediate problems. In these circumstances it is often necessary for something dramatic to happen in order to draw attention to what needs to be done.

At the same time, while accepting that strikes and lock-outs are an intrinsic component of our system of industrial relations; that a certain incidence of strikes is unavoidable; and that such dramatic expressions of conflict can stimulate productive measures for reducing or regulating conflict, we still believe that the large majority of strikes are damaging. They are avoidable and the result of bad management. This is particularly true of the unofficial ones which make up the main body of strikes. They are the result of ill-trained, inadequate supervisors or managers; inadequate procedures for dealing with disputes or grievances and inadequate people on both the management and the trade-union side to deal with disputes quickly and effectively; or inadequate working conditions, and systems of payment that could not have been better calculated for generating grievances and disputes if they had been designed for that purpose.

But it is not the incidence of strikes that interests us primarily. The more substantial and profound deficiences in our industrial relations practice are our chief concern. They permit massive under-employment, that has many of the same damaging effects as unemployment, as well as ensuring low productivity; they inhibit the introduction of change, new techniques, plant and technology; impose conditions, social distinctions and power relationships on workers from which they have long since escaped outside work. These are slum physical conditions of work, terms of employment based on artificial social-class differences, sets of tasks that offer no scope for the use and development of abilities or personal growth, and the acceptance of an unquestioning subordinate position to authority without opportunity for a say over decisions that affect workers directly and critically.

When we talk about employee or industrial relations we are talking not about something that is self-contained or separate from either business or people's lives but rather something that is central to both. We are talking about the management of human resources, which is perhaps the most important aspect of business management, although often the proportion of investment of time, interest, manpower and finance it receives would suggest that it is the least important. However intrinsically offensive it may be to draw analogies between men and machines, this lack of concern can be highlighted by the way in which taking on even the lowest paid machine operator is the equivalent of buying a piece of plant worth £10,000 with a life of ten years. Yet no management would dream of paying as little attention to the purchasing, installation, maintenance and performance of £10,000 worth of plant as it does to the selection, training, motivation and performance of a machine operator. The management of human resources should be a central element of business management alongside if not above the management of finance, production and marketing.

The quality of work and working experience is central to the quality of people's lives. Men spend half their adult working lives at work and women an increasing proportion. What happens at work can be shown to pervade their lives, leisure, patterns of consumption, social and family relationships, standing in the community as well as their standard of life. People have a right to expect and will increasingly come to expect the same standards at work as they have achieved outside work: for instance, the same standards of physical amenities, a narrowing of social-class differences and the exercise of power based on agreement.

Thus improving employee and industrial relations means both increasing business effectiveness and improving the quality of workers' lives. Sometimes the two aims conflict but often they do not. They may even be interdependent and can at least be reconciled in ways that we have described. We have highlighted throughout the report the way in which relationships between groups in business organizations are based upon both differing and common interests. The key both to more effective operation and less overt manifestations of conflict lies in devising mechanisms and institutions for resolving and regulating differences. These include joint problem solving, and the seeking of new, third solutions to serve common interests, in addition to compromise or horse-trading from fixed negotiating positions.

Nevertheless in placing employee relations and the use of human resources in the centre of business management we recognize that they must be reconciled with the other interests and objectives of the enterprise. This will almost certainly ensure that relationships between groups of employees and management in the enterprise can never be sweetness and light or perfect harmony. The demands made upon the enterprise by changes in the market, technological advances and competition, as well as the different groups it serves, ensure that the interests of employees will have to be reconciled with other interests and demands. Equally employees will want to promote and defend their objectives in relation to the other conflicting goals that the business has to serve. Consequently the governing body of the enterprise and its agents, management, will often have to take measures, in response to other demands made upon it, that employees do not like and do not want. It will for instance have to make changes that may make people, jobs or skills redundant and while effective manpower planning, the sharing of information, and the joint development of provisions for redundancy (Daniel and Mukherjee, 1970) can ease the problems for all parties this essentially represents the regulation of conflict rather than its elimination. It will have to say 'no' to demands from employees for a greater share of the wealth generated by the enterprise in order to safeguard the customer and the community from higher prices, or the shareholder from a reduction in the value of his investment and the return it provides, or the enterprise itself from going out of business. Equally as people's own needs and interests are generally more real and immediate to them than those of other parties, employees will be aggrieved when changes happen to damage them and when their claims are turned down in the name of other interests.

This is not to imply that the sole aim of the business enterprise is to produce profit or that all other aims must be subordinated to this, including the quality of employee relations; but any enterprise has a number of interests to serve including those of shareholders, consumers and the general community as well as those of employees, and so it must change, adapt and employ all its resources efficiently. This, in turn, will require at least a sufficiently adequate return on capital to permit investment for the future, whether or not the enterprise is privately or publicly owned.

At the same time in so far as the enterprise assumes the right to take decisions that critically affect the lives, health, wealth, safety and security of its employees, it has a special responsibility to minimize any damaging effects on employees of decisions taken with reference to other interests or demands. Stating that principle is easier than specifying direct guidelines to action that follow from it, but it is a principle that most would share – though again would find it difficult to specify how business decisions have been made, reversed or modified with reference to it, or what cash value can be placed on it.

Given that employee relations and the management of human resources are central to the effective operation of a business, but have to be allotted a place among the over-all interests of the management of the enterprise, three conclusions follow.

First the employee-relations function should be represented at the highest level of decision making in the enterprise which, in the case of all but the smallest firms, means the board. A recent PEP survey of the composition of the boards of major companies shows that this is still true of only 28 per cent of them. (BIM, 1972)

Secondly there is the need to develop a strong, expert, specialist, professional staff function within the organization, under the board member.

Thirdly, and most importantly, it is essential that it be recognized that employee relations and the management of human resources is the direct responsibility of every manager in the enterprise, from the chief executive to the foreman. Moreover the appraisal of his performance should explicitly acknowledge this responsibility and take into account his ability to manage the people subordinate to him. This may seem to be setting a very high standard when the systematic appraisal of any aspect of management performance is so little practised. Unfortunately there can be few companies in which a manager would be penalized for failing to develop his work, team provided that his end results, production or sales figures for instance, were maintained. He is more likely to be rewarded and promoted despite his failure, leaving behind him the heritage of a run-down work group for his successor. In this way a 'high-flyer' leap-frogs his way up an organization, getting apparently good results in each job but only because he is promoted before the effects of a demoralized work team can catch up with him. To take the offensive, mechanical analogy again, nobody is going to thank, reward or promote a manager for running a machine beyond its limits, without adequate servicing or maintenance, in order to achieve impressive short-term re.ults but only at the expense of longer-term breakdowns and cost. But what is ludicrous in terms of the management of plant is happening all the time in the management of men. And this can be changed only through the building into job descriptions of specific responsibilities in this area, the measurement of performance, and the linking of rewards to performance on this criterion as well as others. What all three of these conclusions assume is the paramount importance of management taking a lead in industrial relations, having a policy, setting explicit objectives, planning and critically evaluating its performance. The most striking characteristic of the policy of most companies is that they have none. They are content to react to events and until they become convinced that it is as necessary to manage their labour relations as any other aspect of the business they will remain the victims of events.

But beyond the recognition of the importance of human resource management at board level and beyond the building of this into the job descriptions of every employee with subordinates, the central importance of this area and the special responsibility that employers have for employees has led some employers such as the British Steel Corporation to go a stage further and appoint employee or worker directors. We have reviewed the many arguments for and against this idea in Chapter eight and are unimpressed by the suggestion that the mere existence of workers' directors leads employees to any greater sense of involvement in decision making or involvement in their jobs and the enterprise. Given the general system of industrial relations in Britain we see the chief channel of worker involvement in decision making as being through greater decentralization of decisions and the extension of joint job regulation, joint decision making and collective bargaining. Thus, both the promotion and protection of employee interests and involvement in decision making we see as ultimately dependent upon strong and fully representative employee bodies.

We do not, however, see management and boards representing purely the interests of shareholders, with unions set in permanent opposition. We see the management and the board balancing a number of interests and responsibilities, including those in respect of their employees, and we see employees both directly and through representative bodies contributing to more effective operation and serving common interests as well as opposing where there are conflicts of interest.

Within this framework the idea of workers' directors begins to make more sense and to warrant serious consideration. First, workers' directors would provide the channel for worker involvement in decision making at the highest level, allowing workers to contribute their ideas while policy and decisions were being formulated, rather than merely opposing board decisions. Secondly, such directors would symbolize, to all levels of management and to employees, a full acceptance of the need for greater worker involvement and of the fact that workers have much more to contribute to the running of the enterprise than is at present allowed. Thirdly, unlike the majority of conventional board members, they could more readily understand and identify with the interests of workers. Thus, given that the board seeks to fulfil responsibilities to employees and recognize their interests, it is probable that the quality of its decision making would be improved by an input of people with a very different set of social experiences — provided they were people of high ability prepared to contribute to the board's proceedings. In this sense the argument that workers' directors would improve board decision making by bringing to bear a particular background and experience now lacking appears more persuasive than any suggestion that their appointment would in itself bring about a greater identification of interests between workers and the enterprise.

This introduction has sought to establish a framework within which to locate our more specific conclusions on improvements in employee relations. We have tried to show that good employee relations are separate neither from the running of a business nor from the values on which our society is built. Now we propose to look at what might be considered to be more down-to-earth topics such as physical amenities, job structure and organization, social relationships and involvement, terms of employment and systems of payment. First, however, we must repeat our warning that there are very wide variations in what is appropriate to different organizations. Management's attitude to employee-relations research and innovation is too often unconstructive and ambivalent: on the one hand, there is the categorical assertion that it is impossible to generalize, that each case is unique and no one else's experience can be relevant; on the other, there is a tendency to seek simple little packages of easy answers which will fit all circumstances and solve all problems.

We see no simple package of easy answers universally applicable. At the same time there is no basis for claiming that every enterprise is unique and that it is impossible to make any general statements. It is possible to categorize and analyse, to identify types of enterprise according to different sources of variation, and suggest what is appropriate or how feasible a particular course of action is to different types of situation. Thus, time and again, we have come back to the point that size, technology, market situation, composition and type of labour force and history are important variables. We would like management to develop a more analytical approach, in which it looks critically at its own enterprise, diagnoses what is wrong in order of priority, and evaluates feasible remedies. It should neither reject out of hand any outside experience or findings, nor blindly apply lessons which have proved successful elsewhere without questioning their appropriateness and importance in the over-all set of the things that need to be done.

For instance, we have seen in Section One that job enrichment is feasible in many circumstances and that it can bring substantial benefits for the individual and the enterprise. And we have seen some sense in the Herzberg theory of motivation: that once the context in which a job is done and the conditions of employment in the widest sense are satisfactory, these cease to be salient for employees and what becomes important is the work they do, the content of their jobs and the scope it provides for achievement, interest and responsibility. But even given this analysis it is a nonsense for many employers to preoccupy themselves with job enrichment for manual workers. Leaving aside the question of whether it is feasible or appropriate in their circumstances, and often it will not be, the conditions of employment are often so bad that there is a very long way to go before the extra that might be achieved by whatever little job enrichment is feasible should feature very high in their priorities. If they have slum working conditions, if they have warring relationships between supervisors and men, or a complete breakdown of relationships, if they have a system of payment that is as irrational as it is inequitable, then they have a very great deal to do before they start to think about job enrichment.

Physical conditions and amenities

Concern with our national physical environment has become one of the more fashionable social movements during the first years of the 1970s. Yet what is happening to the countryside, for instance, and the section of our community that is inconvenienced or offended, pales into insignificance compared with the environment in which vast numbers of people pass their working lives. It is a matter of common observance to those unfortunate enough to spend much of their time visiting our factories that many people endure their work in the midst of filth, noise, heat and stench. Of course it is in the nature of many production processes that they are dirty, hot and noisy; but it is not true of by any means all, and in the vast majority such conditions can be alleviated.

But it is not only the workplace which all too often is subject to these conditions. Amenities, too, are poor. Lavatory facilities resemble field latrines, and locker, changing and washing facilities no better. Canteens provide unpalatable food, produced in unhygienic conditions and served on dirty tables standing among dust and ash. The whole picture symbolizes a management that does not care, that has no pride in what it does and is interested only in its own comfort and profit.

We believe that employees have a right to decent physical conditions of work and that management has an obligation to provide them. Where it does not do so it should be pressurized into providing them by employees and their representatives. Rather than being too militant, employees and their representatives have all too often been apathetic and willing to accept the degrading conditions they are subjected to as an inevitable and intrinsic part of work.

Of course, while all too common, such conditions are not universal. Some managements have a completely different approach. They have fully embraced their responsibilities towards employees. They have taken the view that whatever they do should be done as well as possible. The conditions of employment and amenities reflect, they believe, what they are like as managers. If they provide a canteen, then that canteen, the food it serves and its furnishing are the best and this applies to lavatory, washing, changing and locker facilities. They see such care as symbolic of their feeling of responsibility towards employees and a physical manifestation of an over-all management philosophy in which concern for employees is an integral part. They go further than this and expect that it will be seen and interpreted as such by employees, who will respond to this concern by being more emotionally attached to the enterprise and it goals.

Where managements have made a deliberate and concerted attempt to improve their amenities and physical conditions they have often been able to point to an improvement in ease of recruitment, a reduction in labour turnover — with all the ensuing cost reduction in staff recruitment, training and administration that this brings — and an improvement in reputation as an employer among the local community and existing staff.

This is quite consistent with research findings showing that, among many workers, physical conditions of work are an important factor in attracting them to a job, and that their estimation of their employer as an employer is closely linked to the extent to which he goes beyond the minimum that he is required to do. However the expectation that good physical conditions and amenities, on their own, will increase involvement in work is more dubious. Throughout the report we have been concerned to draw a distinction between what workers are interested in, what their priorities are, in different contexts and situations. And in distinguishing between what attracts them to a job, as opposed to what interests and motivates them in the job, or again what predisposes them to leave, we placed physical conditions and amenities as sometimes salient in job choice but very much less so in interest, involvement and motivation.

It may well be that a dramatic change in conditions may produce a short-term variation in response but this is likely to be essentially short-term unless it is backed up by changes in the practice of management. Changes in involvement and motivation must come from something beyond this, particularly social relationships, the treatment employees receive as people, and task content.

Treatment as individuals

Raising the question of how employees are treated as individual people at work can only provoke the answer that all too often they are not. They are treated as units of labour, as costs, as trouble-makers, as obstructions to what managers consider to be their main task. A recurring and persistent theme from employees is that they are treated as tiny cogs in a machine, as ciphers permitted no individuality or identity of their own.

This suggests that management should be more aware of employees as individuals and give them more individual treatment; but the recognition of employees' individuality can mean many things to many people. It can mean the traditional, Hawthorne, human-relations concept of taking an interest in all aspects of the employee's life, being aware of his private and domestic circumstances and problems and aware that these can influence his performance and behaviour at work, and providing personnel services to help him resolve them. It is undoubtedly true that some employees welcome this kind of interest and help, and interpret it as a sign of the employer's concern and respect for them as individuals. It is equally true that many other employees see it not as a recognition of their individuality and identity but an infringement of it. They regard their own personal affairs as their private business, and any attempt by an employer to probe them as an invasion of their privacy and an offence to their dignity and identity. They would prefer that the employer confines himself to what happens at work. Clearly, before seeking to treat employees as individuals, an employer will want to be clear about what type of labour force he has got, and within that labour force what type of individual he is dealing with. Where he provides facilities to help in personal matters of this kind he should make it clear that they are voluntary.

The second sense in which employees can be treated as individuals is in recognizing that they have ideas, interests, abilities and aptitudes that are unique to them: ideas about how their job should be done and how the organization they work in should be run; ideas and feelings about changes that are taking place around them. And treating them as individuals involves giving them an opportunity to express these ideas and see some results. In the same sense people can be treated as individuals by giving them the opportunity both to do jobs that are most closely in line with their interests and abilities, and to develop themselves, and be developed for, those that coincide with their aptitudes.

Thirdly, people can be treated as individuals by appraising their performance individually and rewarding merit or penalizing shortcomings on an individual basis.

This however highlights the fact that problems arise from treating people as individuals, and constraints and limitations also. The first is the problem of size.

Certainly, in so far as there are any laws of organization, one is that increasing size leads to greater bureaucratization. Size demands more formulation of procedures, and the concept of equity becomes with size increasingly related to conforming to agreed rules and procedures rather than individual need. Thus, in an organization where everybody knows everybody and their circumstances, it is possible for some people to get to work consistently late, or to take time off frequently, and for this to be acceptable, and accepted as equitable, because of the particular circumstances or needs. As an organization increases in size, however, it becomes necessary to specify times when people have to arrive, circumstances under which they can be absent from work, and for sanctions for absenteeism and lateness to be consistently and uniformly applied. Thus with size the balance between the application of standard procedures and the treatment of employees as individuals begins to change to greater emphasis on the former. It becomes more difficult to treat employees as individuals and conscious policies and procedures have to be developed and implemented to ensure this still happens.

Ultimately this may involve the recognition that economies of scale have their ceilings. This is just one of the reasons why many large employers who think seriously about the way that they manage people are taking practical steps to decentralize, not only in terms of procedures and levels of decision making but also in terms of reinforcing these by the spatial and physical location of plant: they have set limits on the size of any single unit they operate and the number of people they employ on any one site. While, for instance, in the production of steel, economies of size are overwhelmingly attractive, in many other technologies the benefits of economies in size have to be balanced against losses. One loss is certainly a decline in the sense of identity and involvement among employees. It is, of course, very difficult to draw up a convincing balance sheet demonstrating how the higher overheads generated by imposing ceilings on the number of people employed on any one site are outweighed by the benefits this brings. However, experience has convinced an increasing proportion of employers that the benefits of having, firstly, a small, closely knit, unified management team sharing a common philosophy and aims and secondly a greater sense of involvement and higher morale among the workforce and thirdly more constructive labour relations, fully justify the costs. What this demonstrates, however is that in order to treat people as individuals it is necessary to devize conscious policies and make special provision, which may have a cost as well as a benefit, if the aim is to be anything more than a slogan.

The second problem about individual treatment is that, however much people want to be treated as individuals, however much they see themselves as unique, and however much they regard their identity and individuality as sacred, they do not always behave as individuals. They are also members of groups and they behave as such. The groups of which they are members have their own ideas of what is desirable or undesirable behaviour and individuals conform to a greater or lesser extent to what the group demands. This has become a cliché in organizational analysis ever since the Hawthorne Bank Wiring Observation Room work group analysis. But it remains true of very many industrial work groups. And it is no good paying people individual incentives if they immediately turn them into group payment schemes. There is little point in imposing individual sanctions for loss of production or faulty work if these are paid out of a pool funded by the work groups, as they frequently are. What is necessary is to understand the working of the group in relation to the task it is doing and relate management practice to this. In terms of employee individuality this means that it is as important for the employer to recognize that employees derive as much, if not more, of their identity and self-respect from the acceptance and approval of the work group of which they are a member as they do from their treatment by management.

The third problem about individual treatment concerns the relationship between management and labour. As we have stressed throughout the report the chief strength of employees in circumstances of conflict of interest with management lies in collective pressure based on solidarity. The danger inherent in what passes as respect for the individual, and treatment of employees as individuals, is that it can be and is seen quite consciously by management as a stratagem for undermining group solidarity and weakening collective strength. Management discussions, for instance, on the possibility of introducing individual merit bonuses, often quite consciously take this into account. But, given the nature of the work groups in organizations where this type of consideration is articulated, it is likely that such work groups will quickly find means of countering this strategy and making it counter-productive. For instance the merit bonus may rapidly become a source of wage drift as bargaining pressure puts everyone on the highest rate.

Worker involvement

The allocation of space in our report, and the five chapters we devote to it in Section Two, emphasizes the extent to which we believe that few changes are more important for the achievement of constructive employee relations than greater worker involvement in decision making. But, as we have also emphasized, there is no single mechanism, change or institution that will usher in a new era of industrial democracy. Many different media must be developed at different levels, all requiring hard and painstaking work on the part of management, but we conclude that their healthy development needs to be based on the acceptance by management of three fundamental precepts.

1. Employees at all levels have far more to contribute to the efficient running of the enterprise in which they work than they are currently encouraged to contribute.

2. Any management prerogative to manage is ultimately based on the agreement of the managed and increasingly management will have to earn and will that agreement rather than claim it as of right by virtue of its position.

3. Where trade unions are recognized the union must be the chief channel of involvement and representation of employees, and all media for participation should be developed within the framework of trade union representation and under joint management/ union agreement. This in turn means that rather than adopting the position that their sole role is to question, challenge and oppose management where its interests do or can conflict with their own, trade unionists must also increasingly play a positive, creative role in joint decision making towards common goals. In so far as employees have both common and differing interests with employers, no single body that only opposes can adequately represent the interests of employees; and if the trade union is to be the chief channel of involvement and representation – and where it has negotiating rights we see no constructive alternative at present – then it must seek to play, and be encouraged by

management to play, a fuller part in areas of common interests as well as being permitted to oppose in areas of conflicting interests. On the basis of these three basic propositions we have described in some detail the following media for greater worker involvement, in addition to what is common at present:

1. Greater autonomy and control over tasks in the workplace and the actual job through job enrichment;

2. total involvement exercises in the event of major change through joint working and co-ordinating groups backed up by departmental or shop-floor discussion groups;

3. the development of the habit of consulting, talking and listening through the establishment of integrated institutions for negotiation and consultation and the extension of joint regulation through such media as joint committees for training, manpower planning, productivity, safety and discipline;

4. the use of employee-attitude surveys based on joint control and used as a basis for joint decisions for change;

5. the possibility that the commitment to these changes might be crowned by the appointment of workers' directors.

One feature that we have mentioned less specifically than might have been expected is that of communications. This is not because we think it unimportant, quite the contrary. The importance of good communications is implicit in all that we have written on involvement. But also implicit is our criticism of what so often passes as good communications. This is all too often seen as unilateral, one-way communication, in which management passes on to employees information which it wants them to believe or wants them to hear. We are more interested in two-way communications, creating situations in which employees can question and challenge information and demand more, where they can discuss and evaluate information in an uninhibited way. This is why we see the shop-floor discussion group as such an effective medium for communication and also the Industrial Society's variation on this, the regular briefing session throughout the organization. We see information

being useless, not understood, or misunderstood unless it is related
to action; thus the starting point is new departures such as extended
joint regulation and joint decision making which in turn demand full
in_ormation and good communications.

Perhaps, however intrinsically unimportant it may seem, the
house journal symbolizes for us bad 'good communications'. This
purports to be a channel of information and involvement. In fact,
while there are variations in quality and some notable exceptions,
the house journal is usually a management-controlled, public-
relations machine and is seen and ignored as such. If we use the term
'industrial democracy', and draw a political analogy, it is as if the
BBC were wholly controlled by the government and used solely for
putting out government propaganda, information that the government wants the people to believe in the way it wants it to be
believed, spiced with harmless items of trivia and gossip.

Much more appropriate to the type of relationship we are
suggesting would be a house journal edited by an independent editor
with full freedom and answerable to a joint management/union
committee. He would produce the journal, reporting and com-
menting upon the real news in the organization, including criticism
of management from any sections of the workforce, as well as
editorial criticism. A journal with some life of this kind would have
more chance of being read, and the messages management wants
received more chance of being received, if criticism of management
were included.

We stress this point not because we think house journals are a
particularly significant part of communications or employee relations, but because their present control and editing sums up how far
away is any genuine idea of industrial democracy, and how
persistently many managements cling unthinkingly to what in
outside political and social contexts would be readily recognized as
authoritarian and dictatorial.

Task content and job enrichment

We find it difficult to exaggerate the importance, in discussing
employee relations and involvement in work, of the tasks that
people are required to perform at work. It is, for instance, nonsense
to talk of treating people as individuals if the jobs they are required
to do strip them not only of any individuality or identity but even

of any humanity. And all too often they do. People are denied any freedom, control or meaning in their work or any opportunity to use or develop their own ideas, abilities, interests and aptitudes. Equally, when talking of worker involvement in decision making, the involvement that workers most value and seek most spontaneously is some control over their immediate activities and circumstances in the workplace.

Thus we find the case for job enrichment, for injecting into jobs more scope for interest, for the use and development of abilities, for personal growth and advancement, quite overwhelming. First because it is a recognition of the dignity and humanity of the worker. Secondly because it is critical to his involvement in his job. For these reasons we believe that the onus lies squarely on the practitioners of job impoverishment to demonstrate that any alternative is impossible rather than on the advocates of job enrichment to demonstrate that it is desirable.

In Chapters One and Two we have been able to describe some impressive findings suggesting that job enrichment is feasible in a wide variety of jobs and does bring about more involved and effective employees. At the same time we have identified in Chapter Three some major misunderstandings in management of what it is possible to achieve through job enrichment among manual workers. There seems to be a constant, if illusory and self-defeating, search among many managements for some strategy whereby they can, overnight, convert or transform industrial workers into what they traditionally regard as good, loyal, white-collar workers. Whether they are thinking of treating people as individuals, or granting industrial workers staff status or job enrichment, they seem to be searching for this magic key which will turn industrial workers into something that, given the reality of their social experience and situation and of their interests and expectations, they are incapable of becoming.

We have described how some managers have argued that to create more interesting and rewarding jobs would wean workers away from attachments to trade unions, from ideas of collective advancement and from putting in wage demands. Similarly managements have thought that if they could devise productivity agreements that offered the possibility of enriched jobs then such agreements would become attractive. We have demonstrated the fallacies in these arguments, and have shown how productivity agreements that promised and, in the event, delivered enriched jobs were strongly resisted in the negotiating context and how the benefits were experienced only after implementation. We have highlighted the importance of distinguishing between what interests people in different contexts and situations. Equally we have demonstrated that many workers have a clear insight into the way that ultimately their own advancement is based on the advancement of the group of which they are members and that scope for personal advancement is strictly limited. Through this we have seen how workers place a high value on group solidarity and loyalty and are prepared to deny themselves individual rewards in the name of collective interests.

In order to manage effectively management has to understand and come to terms with this kind of reality rather than try to transform people into something that they are not and cannot be. If management does not do so then concepts such as job enrichment, that offer scope for benefits to both management and employees, will only be devalued and denigrated. Managements will become disillusioned when they do not achieve the impossible; and workers and trade unionists will be antagonistic and resistant, seeing valuable innovations as stratagems designed to undermine their strength and interests.

Although we have been able to point to job enrichment applications across a wide range of jobs, it is clear that there are limitations to its applicability. Most of the more successful applications are limited to either white-collar jobs or, among industrial workers, to jobs in advanced-technology industries such as heavy chemical production and oil refining. Even here, among industrial workers, there is one essential missing component in the job enrichment package: scope for personal advancement, which remains perhaps the biggest single differentiating factor between blue- and white-collar jobs, and a critical source of variation in attachment to and involvement in work. This does not reduce the need for managements to examine the situations in which they find themselves and study the scope that these provide for job enrichment. What it does mean is that they should do so without any illusions that everything is going to be transformed over-night and all their problems will disappear. We emphasize that they should do so in co-operation with workers and their representatives, rather than impose a grand job enrichment package from above, claiming to be the best judges of workers' interests. This is a denial of one of the basic tenets of job enrichment, which is that the man nearest the job often best knows what needs to be done.

Conditions of employment and staff status

In considering terms and conditions of employment the one point that has pre-occupied us is how, for enormous sections of British industry, the hours you work, the way you are paid, the fringe benefits you receive, the pension you qualify for (or do not as the case may be), the notice you receive, your sick pay, the food you eat and where you eat it, the rules you have to conform to and the way you are controlled depend not on your value or contribution to the enterprise, not upon the responsibility you carry or the demands of your job and not even upon the type of work you do. They depend upon whether or not, historically, your job has been associated with brainwork or manual work. They are based on a historical distinction between units of labour, eminently disposable and replaceable, and between valued, loyal servants of the enterprise. The division of employees into staff and works' employees, and the provision of dramatically different amenities and conditions of employment for the different groups, is a social anachronism of which there can be no defence in reason or equity. And moreover if management treats workers as sub-human, fit only for sub-human amenities, with their every action monitored and controlled, it cannot be surprised if this is the way they seem to behave.

At the same time there seems to be little pressure on management to do anything about removing these invidious distinctions. Manual workers' unions seem all too happy to accept them and, if they seek to have them removed, this is very low in their list of priorities. In this they almost certainly reflect the views of their members, who, even if they seek common status in terms and conditions of employment, again place this low in their priorities. Indeed there is evidence that management and supervision are more concerned about the distinctions and more keen to have them removed than workers themselves (Wedderburn, 1969). We have seen how low the staff status elements ranked in our case studies of productivity-agreement evaluation. The economic cost to management of removing them is high. In many cases it would add some 12 to 15 per cent to labour costs immediately; and there is no indication that there would by any corresponding reduction in demands for straight wage increases. Moreover there are tangential costs: demands from white-collar workers for increases to maintain differentials and the possibility of an increase in sickness and absenteeism rates. Nor is there much basis for supposing that management's expectations of gain from such changes have any sound basis. Certainly there are no grounds for believing that merely granting people staff status will suddenly make them embrace attitudes that they have traditionally associated with staff. Distinctions and social differences will remain. The nature of people's jobs will require some people to wear different clothes from others, some to work shifts and overtime and others not, and patterns of social mixing off the job will continue to conform to those required by the job. Similarly differences in the distribution of power and financial rewards will remain.

Given this background there seems very little reason why management should not be content to continue to accept an irrational, invidious situation just as the majority of workers and trade unionists do. But we believe that there remain powerful reasons why this should not be. First, for quite simple, moral reasons, management should not perpetuate a situation that it recognizes to be irrational and inequitable. Second, it must keep ahead or abreast of events; status harmonization is on its way and management is always well advised to think and plan ahead for changes that it knows will happen, rather than be overtaken by events and taken by surprise by demands that it is singularly ill-equipped to deal with. Thirdly, as status harmonization becomes more widespread, so demands can be expected to rise. Although irrational and inequitable distinctions can be accepted as part of the inevitable order of things in a stable situation, they are always a potential source of grievance, frustration and disruption, and they will become more so as people become increasingly aware that they can be ehanged.

Finally, we believe that these distinctions are quite inconsistent with the kind of relationship between managements and employees that we have been advocating throughout this report. If we are to move to a constructive relationship between management and labour, if employees are to be treated by management as individuals, if management is to recognize and make use of the unique insight into their jobs that most employees have, and if it is going to speak and listen to employees on equal terms, then it is inconsistent for one group of employees to be identified as inferior and incapable of exercising self-control in their terms and conditions of employment. Indeed it seems unlikely that this could happen. In short, if the basis of decision making is moving towards increased joint regulation, it would seem reasonable that the status relationship should change to facilitate this. Introducing staff status on its own will not achieve anything, but a perpetuation of prevailing practice is likely to inhibit the development of other desirable forms of change. The granting of staff status, in our view, is more important as a symbol of management attitudes and a means of encouraging a different attitude to labour, rather than as a means of affecting workers' attitudes.

While on balance these arguments make the case for us as regards management taking action to bring about harmonization they do not take into account the immediate cost, which can be heavy. Management has various choices. It can make steps towards harmonization part of a package of changes where management and labour together set about achieving greater efficiency and labour productivity, which will help to finance the improved benefits for workers. This was how the changes were achieved in ICI, BP and Shell. Alternatively the changes can be introduced gradually but progressively and the costs taken fully into account in wage negotiations. What is certainly needed is a clear plan for change, a commitment to it, and a rigorous analysis of the means whereby it can be brought about.

In order to provide a hard basis for the discussion on terms and conditions of employment we have tended to focus very much on the 'staff status' issue with its assumptions that the only question is whether or not manual workers should be given the same terms and conditions of employment as staff. This in fact is not the assumption from which we are working. Our view is better represented by the term 'harmonization' than by the phrase 'staff status for workers'. We are primarily concerned that the total system of remuneration, including wages and salaries, as well as terms and conditions of employment, should be rational and accepted as equitable, that similar criteria should be applied to all sections of the workforce in determining their total remuneration and that what is appropriate should be determined by an analysis of the facts, rather than by assumptions and traditions. Thus we do not accept that staff conditions are ideal and appropriate to all. The nature of many staff jobs is changing. Staff are beginning to want more say in determining their own destinies. There are going to be major changes here too. So it is not just a matter of upgrading manual workers but of devising new harmonized patterns of remuneration and representation.

Systems of payment

Whatever else is important about employees' attachments to work and their feelings about the total concept that is a job, there is no question but that money is enormously important. This is true of both the intrinsic value of earnings and their symbolic value. Thus not only does man work to live but, in our society, what he earns in relation to others is often seen as a direct measure of his worth to others.

Yet as we describe in Chapter nine there are few things more chaotic in many sectors of industry than the system by which people are paid. There are still situations where a group of people all doing very similar types of work, all receive different rates of pay, with the only possible reason for the differences being the preferences of the boss. Overtime is still widely worked not because it needs to be worked but because low base rates have to be supplemented by high overtime to retain and attract staff, so that people spend half the day hanging around doing nothing in order to generate adequate overtime. In this type of situation any talk of efficiency, the effective use of human resources, or virtually any of the other topics that we have discussed is a mockery.

Industry is beset by irrational, fragmented systems of payment which do little but generate grievances, cause disputes and effectively manage the business. Cash piece-rates ensure that the wage system is settled at the lowest level of the hierarchy between the supervisor or rate fixer and the worker or shop steward, that there is a steady and consistent wage drift that nobody can control, that every change, both major and minor, is a source of dispute and resistance and that every supervisor puts off any change in the hope that somebody else will carry it out.

Often at the heart of a major strike will be found this type of payment system: low base rates paid at an enormous number of different rates, supplemented by a maze of plussages, and premium payments, the origins of many of which are lost in the mists of time, which are understood by few, if any, and can be justified by none. Thus perhaps the most important aspect of personnel management is irrational, inequitable, and completely out of the hands of management.

Having identified the problem however, the possible solutions are a little more complex. The difficulties can be highlighted by examining the numerous aims that a payment system should serve. Management may want it to reward and stimulate effort, to promote stability and security, to give the employee a steady income without wild fluctuations, to be simple and easily understood, to be rational and equitable, and not give rise to anomalous variations in earnings between groups of employees and individuals, variations that bear no relationship to job content or effort, to minimize disputes and grievances, to link the futures of employees with that of the enterprise, and to commit employees to the enterprise. Clearly all these objectives cannot be served at the same time. Any direct incentive or reward system is in danger of throwing up anomalies, fluctuations in earnings, grievances and disputes. But, at the same time, whether or not an incentive scheme operates as an incentive, the idea that differing levels of effort should be differentially rewarded has an enduring basis in concepts of equity at many levels.

Increasingly, however, the trend seems to be towards high, stable, base rates deriving from job evaluation and work measurement. We have stressed how job evaluation is important because it is a truism that disputes about wages and earnings are almost invariably about differentials. Systematic job evaluation seeks to establish an agreed basis for comparing different jobs and measuring the differing values. There are different systems, of ranging merit; some of the criteria are objective, others are based on value judgements. It is possible to describe and measure the content of many jobs with some exactitude; and it is possible to measure the different qualities that are required to do the job with some exactitude. But when it comes to the value that should be placed upon the different qualities – stress, physical effort, skill, training or aptitude – then it becomes more a matter of judgement and values. Some managements have tended to take the view that in job evaluation they have an exact, scientific instrument and that its findings and conclusions are inviolate. It would be more honest and productive if they recognized that what they are seeking is a rational systematic way of comparing and evaluating jobs in relation to some common denominator of equity. And, in so far as there are value judgements, there is room for genuine disagreement and a need to discuss and reconcile differences. All the work that we have done suggests that the success of a job-evaluation system is directly linked to the degree of union and worker involvement in its design and implementation.

Linked to the job-evaluation system increasingly is a relatively stable, or even, flat rate. In advanced technology this is increasingly becoming a fixed salary with no variations. In engineering it may increasingly become a fixed rate linked to performance such as in the Philips premium payment plan or IMB merit banding systems, where workers can progress up a gradient of fixed rates according to performance. Alternatively it may be a simple, measured, day-work system in which earnings are stabilized but work load is established and agreed by work measurement.

Increasingly then management is coming less to rely on its system of payment to do its management for it, providing instead stable earnings based upon systematic assessment, and relying upon its managers to manage.

This area, however, is one where we base great reliance upon joint regulation. We have highlighted the way in which piece-work systems have tended to get out of management control and be controlled on the shop floor. And the one aspect of piece-work incentives that workers do value is the scope that these give for control. Each man can see himself as an entrepreneur, or his own boss, in which he sells as many pieces as he likes to make, at the best price he can negotiate. He can produce more when he wants to and less when he does not. Thus, what was initially seen by trade unionists as a system that divided the work group and tied the man to production become a source of workers' control. If management wants to change this situation and recover control then it can best do so by sharing control and by seeking change through agreement and joint regulation.

Tailpiece

Given the extreme diversity of industrial and business enterprise, it is enormously difficult to produce a report on employee relations that is generally applicable without being platitudinous and too abstract to provide any guidelines for action. Our concern therefore has been to focus mainly on that sector of industry where we believe that change is most urgently required and to identify trends for the future.

If there is a constant theme in our report it is that the relationship between management and employees is based upon varying degrees of common and differing interests. There is a tendency among management and employers to accentuate common interests and to deny or fail to see differences in interests. This is essentially because it is in management's interest to have employees see their interests as identical with management. This legitimizes management's power and its right to make decisions unilaterally and it seeks to sustain the *status quo* by charging anyone who seeks change apart from management as being a trouble maker, militant or someone threatening the good of all groups in the enterprise.

Equally, there is a tendency for trade unionists to focus upon differences in interests. This is partly because they are cast in the role of opposition and too often are allowed to have a say, or are provoked to demand a say, only in situations of conflict of interest. It is also partly due to the fact that given that their members are so often the 'have-nots' under the present system, being at the bottom of the structure of power, status and reward, having the lowest earnings, the least interesting and rewarding jobs, the least expectation of growth and advancement, and the least formal say over decisions in the enterprise, the unions have the greater interest in challenging and changing the present system.

We have highlighted the way in which a more constructive relationship between management and employees can be forged by management recognizing that there are differences of interests as well as common ones — as employees and trade unionists tend to see rather more clearly — and permitting employees through trade unions to have a greater say in the running of the enterprise. We stress that this should be through trade unions because for the main body of industry where change needs to be generated, unions are fully recognized, and the alternative to the union being the chief channel of representation in all matters is the union being cast in a purely obstructive, destructive and opposition role.

All this requires that management recognize that it manages only with the agreement of the managed. It does not take decisions as of right because of its position, but must justify that right by demonstrating professional and technical expertise, and by demonstrating that the decisions are in the interests of employees. This involves giving information, consulting, discussing and seeking agreement. It involves recognizing employees' interests, ideas and abilities and the possibility that their understanding of the enterprise through their jobs can contribute to better decisions. Thus it is not communication or consultation in a paternalistic or patronizing way that are needed but rather talking and listening to people as equals. All too often in considerations of communication it is the critical importance of listening that is ignored.

But to bring these changes about there is also a need for a major change among trade unions. There are the obvious needs for trade-union representatives to become better trained, more professional, in order to deal with this new role. Trade-union systems of communication have often not even reached the stage of management's formal system of unilateral communication that we have found so inadequate. In particular, given the need for trade unionists to become more heavily involved in joint decision making at the level of the enterprise, which essentially means ordinary trade-union members and lay officers becoming thus involved, then they need the backing of many more expert, full-time officers who are able to supply technical and financial servicing and ensure that their increased involvement is not at the expense of their interests. But, beyond all these more obvious changes, there is a need for trade unions to broaden the basis of their platform. For far too long they have been content to limit their interests to earnings. Partly this is because this is the only role they have been permitted by management. Partly it is a genuine reflection of their members' priorities, or at least achieving an increase in earnings is something concrete and specific that demonstrates to their members that they are fulfilling some useful function. But this is not enough. In many ways the situation prevailing in industry, the poverty of job content, the appalling physical conditions and amenities, the lack of opportunity for workers to have a say over events, the invidious and anomalous class distinction in conditions of employment, are as much an indictment of trade-union failure as of management failure. Trade unions should thus increasingly press for changes in these areas too if they are adequately to represent the interests of their members. This is beginning to happen. Unions are beginning to become more active in seeking a greater sharing of power and control. As in the case of Fiat and Renault they are beginning to say 'no' to damaging, destructive, impoverished jobs. In so far as we are seeking change, and trade union pressure is one of the sources of change, such pressure is to be welcomed.

Finally, in many of the specific areas that we have looked at in detail — job enrichment, involvement in decision making and participative styles of management, status harmonization and simple salaried systems of payment — have been taken furthest in enterprises based upon advanced technology or automation, heavy chemicals and oil although there are notable exceptions in other sectors. But this we would suggest is the trend. These enterprises are setting the pace and both social and technological change suggest that these are the directions in which industry should move.

Sources and References

Adamson, W.C. (1970), *C.B.I. Director General's inaugural letter to members.*

Argyris, C. (1964), *Integrating the Individual and the Organization,* Wiley, New York.

Bain, G.S. (1967), *Trade Union Growth and Recognition,* Research Paper No. 6 for the Donovan Commission H.M.S.O., London.

Bean, R. and Garside, D.A. (1971), *Payment by Results Systems: Some indicators of incidence of and relevance to capital intensive operations,* B.J.I.R., Vol. 9, No. 2

Blauner, R. (1960), *Work Satisfaction and Industrial Trends,* in Galenson, W. and Lipset, S.M. (eds.), *Labour and Trade Unionism,* Wiley, New York.

Blumberg, P. (1968), *Industrial Democracy: The Sociology of Participation,* Constable, London.

Blumenthal, W.M. (1956), *Co-determination in the German Steel Industry,* Princeton University Press.

Bolle DeBal, M. (1970), *Plant Bonus Systems-Theory and Practice of Plant Bonus Systems,* O.E.C.D., Paris.

C.I.R. Report No. 14, *Standard Telephones and Cables Ltd.,* Cmnd. 4598, H.M.S.O., London.

C.I.R. Report No. 17, *Facilities Afforded to Shop Stewards,* Cmnd. 4668, H.M.S.O., London.

Clegg, H.A. (1960), *A New Approach to Industrial Democracy,* Blackwell, Oxford.

Coates, K.ed. (1971), *A Trade Union Strategy in the Common Market,* Spokesman Books, Nottingham.

Coch, L. and French, J.R.P. (1948), *Overcoming Resistance to Change,* Human Relations No. 1, London.

Corina, J. (1970), *Forms of Wage and Salary Payment for High Productivity,* O.E.C.D., Paris.

Cotgrove, S., Dunham, J and Vanplew, C. (1971), *The Nylon Spinners,* Allen and Unwin, London.

Cousins, J.(1972), *The Non-Militant Shop Steward,* New Society, No. 488.

Dahrendorf, R. (1959), *Class and Class Conflict in Industrial Society,* Routledge and Kegan Paul, London.

Dalziel, S. and Klein, L. (1960), *The Human Implications of Work Study,* Dept. of Scientific and Industrial Research, London.

Daniel, W.W. (1970a), *Beyond the Wage Work Bargain,* PEP Broadsheet 519, London.

Daniel, W.W. (1970b), It still pays to make productivity deals, The Times, 28, September

Donovan, (1968), *Royal Commission on Trade Unions and Employers Associations,* Cmnd. 3623, H.M.S.O., London.

Emery, F.E. and Thorsrud, E. (1969), *Form and Content in Industrial Democracy,* Tavistock, London.

Flanders, A. (1964), *The Fawley Productivity Agreements,* Faber and Faber, London.

Flanders, A. (1967), *Collective Bargaining: Prescription for Change,* Faber and Faber, London.

Fogarty, M. (1969), *Worker Representation on Company Boards: A discussion,* Industrial, Educational and Research Foundation.

Ford, R.N. (1969), *Motivation through the work itself,* American Management Association, New York.

Fox, A. (1966), *The Time Span of Discretion Theory: An appraisal,* Institute of Personnel Management, London.

Gallup Poll (1969), *Awareness and Attitudes to Workers' Participation*, London.

Goldstein, J. (1952), *The Government of British Trade Unions*, Allen and Unwin, London.

Goldthorpe, J.H., Lockwood, D., Bechofer, F. and Platt, J. (1970), *The Affluent Worker: Industrial Attitudes and Behaviour*, Cambridge University Press.

Government Social Survey, (1968), *Workplace Industrial Relations*, H.M.S.O., London.

Griffiths, W. and Jones, K. (1971), *Employee Involvement in Management: The B.S.C. Experiment*, Co-partnership (November).

Grinyer, P. and Kessler, S. (1967), *The Systematic Evaluation of Methods of Wage Payment*, Journal of Management Studies, Vol. 4, No. 3, London.

Henderson, J. (1970), *Some Examples of Effective Consultative Committees*, The Industrial Society, London.

Herzberg, F., Mausner, B. and Snyderman, B.B. (1959), *The Motivation to Work*, Wiley, New York.

Hickson, D. (1963), *Worker Choice of Payment System*, Occupational Psychology, Vol. 37, No. 2, London.

Hughes, J. (1968), *Trade Union Structure and Government*, Research Paper 5 (part 2) for Donovan Commission, H.M.S.O., London.

Jacques, E. (1961), *Equitable Payment*, Heinemann, London.

Jones, K. (1971), *Involvement in Decision Making*, Co-partnership (January), London.

King, A. (1964), *From Group Bonus to Wage Consolidation*, Industrial Welfare (October), London.

Klein, L. (1964), *Multi Products Ltd: A case study on the social effects of rationalized production*, H.M.S.O., London.

Likert, R. (1961), *New Patterns of Management*, McGraw-Hill, New York.

Lupton, T, (1969), in D.Pym, ed., *Industrial Society, Social Sciences in Management,* Penguin, London.

Lupton, T. and Gowler, D. (1969), *Selecting a Wage Payment System,* E.E.F. Research Paper No. 3, London.

Marriot, R. (1961), *Incentives: A Review of Research and Opinion,* Staples, London.

Maslow, A.H. (1970), *Motivation and Personality,* 2nd. edition, Harper and Row, New York.

McGregor, D. (1960), *The Human side of Enterprise,* McGraw-Hill, New York.

McGregor, D. (1966), *Leadership and Motivation,* M.I.T., Cambridge, Mass.

Mopham, G.J. (1964), *Philips Premium Pay Plan,* Industrial Welfare (August), London.

N.B.P.I. (1968), Report No. 65, *Payment by Results Systems,* H.M.S.O., London.

N.B.P.I. (1968), Report No. 83, *Job Evaluation,* H.M.S.O., London.

Nelson-Jones, J. (1971), *The Wages of Fear,* Bow Group, London.

North, D.T.B. and Buckingham, G.L. (1969), *Productivity Agreements and Wage Systems,* Gower Press London.

Parsons, R.I. (1966), *The Premium Pay Plan,* Philips Industries, London.

Paul, W.J. and Robertson, K.B. (1971), *Job Enrichment and Employee Motivation,* Gower Press, London.

Paynter, W. (1970), *British Trade Unions and the Problem of Change,* Allan and Unwin, London.

Philips, *Work Structuring: a summary of experiments at Philips,* 1963–68, Philips, Eindhoven.

Roberts, B.C. (1956), *Trade Union Government and Adminstration in Great Britain,* Bell, London.

Roethlisberger, F. and Dixon, W.J. (1964), *Management and the Worker,* Wiley, New York.

Shenfield, B. (1970), *Company Boards,* PEP, Allen and Unwin, London.

Shephard, G.C. (1970), *Worker Participation in Coal-Mining,* Co-partnership (October), London.

Shimmin, S. (1959), *Payment by Results: A Psychological Investigation,* Staples Press, London.

Spiro, H. (1958), *The Politics of Co-Determination,* Harvard University Press, Cambridge, Mass.

Tabb, J.Y. and Goldfarb, A. (1966), *Workers' Participation in Management,* Pergamon Press, London.

Transport and General Workers Union, (1971), *The Ford Wage Claim,* a T.G.W.U. pamphlet.

Trist, E.L. et al. (1963), *Organizational Choice,* Tavistock, London.

Turner, H.A., Clack, G. and Roberts, G. (1967), *Labour Relations in the Motor Industry,* Allen and Unwin, London.

Wedderburn, D. (1968), The conditions of employment of manual and non-manual workers in the Proceedings of an SSRC conference: social stratification and industrial relations, Cambridge University.